GUIDE TO RECORDING HISTORIC BUILDINGS

D1610741

ICOMOS

BUT

London   Boston   Singapore   Sydney   Toronto   Wellington

Butterworth Architecture
is an imprint of Butterworth-Heinemann

 PART OF REED INTERNATIONAL P.L.C.

First published 1990

© **International Council on Monuments and Sites, 1990**

British Library Cataloguing in Publication Data

Guide to recording historic buildings.
1. Buildings of historical importance. Recording.
I. International Council on Monuments and Sites.
363.69

ISBN 0-7506-1210-X

Library of Congress Cataloging-in-Publication Data

Guide to recording historic buildings / ICOMOS.
   p.   cm.
ISBN 0-7506-1210-X:
1. Historic buildings – Documentation – United States.
I. International Council on Monuments and Sites.
E159.G83   1990
363.6'9'0723–dc20   90-2546

Photoset by Latimer Trend & Company Ltd, Plymouth
Printed in Great Britain at the University Press, Cambridge

CONTENTS

FOREWORD by HRH The Duke of Gloucester

ACKNOWLEDGEMENTS

INTRODUCTION   Purposes of recording   1

Chapter 1   WHY? Objectives of recording   3
Chapter 2   WHEN? Occasions for recording   10
Chapter 3   WHAT? Features that require recording   25
Chapter 4   HOW? Approaches and techniques   32
Chapter 5   WHO? Carrying out the initial survey   67
Chapter 6   WHERE? Preserving the record   69

Appendix I   Interpretative elements   73
Appendix II   Some useful addresses   77

FOREWORD

by HRH The Duke of Gloucester, GCVO

Patron

The International Council on Monuments and Sites

We are fortunate in Britain to have a very rich supply of historic buildings; not only great churches and public buildings, but also many mundane buildings preserved over the centuries as family homes.

In a period of rapid change these solid landmarks have been ever more greatly valued, not only by those who occupy them, but also by those for whom their familiarity confirms a sense of place, individuality and continuity with the past.

It has always been man's instinct to make his home as comfortable as possible, and the mellow stone walls of many a medieval cottage have benefited from modern methods of keeping out the damp that was an inevitable cohabitant for the first few hundred years of occupation.

The historic buildings we can still see today are those which have been most successfully adapted to new and changing uses over the time since their construction; the short lived have been replaced by more useful buildings. Today the survivors are less threatened by wholesale destruction than in any previous era, but as monuments to the methods and practices of the past they are under threat, even from those who live in them and love them, and are 'improving' them by making them more efficient, more insulated, more weather tight, or by heightening doors that forced taller generations to duck. Each change takes them further from their creators and diminishes our proof of the reality of the past.

It is not the thesis of this book that such practice should be discouraged, but rather that its significance can be understood if each change can be recorded and explained.

Historians research into ideas and the influence of people on each other, but architectural historians research into buildings; their understanding is in construction and how it developed over the centuries with new techniques and materials. Their knowledge has grown in response to public interest in preserving our built heritage, yet every year more and more of the past is buried or destroyed as old buildings are repaired or adapted by people unaware of the significance of their labours.

This book is intended to draw attention both to the need for recording such changes as well as the methods that should be used. If it should prove effective, then succeeding generations will be able to deduce much more from these living monuments to our past. It will I hope also open the eyes of many occupants of historic houses and give them a greater understanding and appreciation of their homes and that feeling of being responsible for our past for the sake of our future.

ACKNOWLEDGEMENTS

This book has been prepared by a committee set up by the ICOMOS UK executive in 1987, under the chairmanship of Robert Chitham, to consider the guidance on recording available to those involved in the care of historic buildings. Because notoriously the products of committees are not noted for their elegant design, the preparation of the text was entrusted to a single member of the committee, Nicholas Cooper of the Royal Commission on the Historical Monuments of England. Whilst the contributions of the committee as a whole should not be overlooked, it is to a great extent due to his sustained effort that it has been completed in the form it displays. In the selection and preparation of the illustrations he was greatly assisted by Mike Sutherill of the Historic Buildings and Monuments Commission for England (English Heritage).

Acknowledgements are due to the following for permission to reproduce the illustrations in the guide:

Plates 6, 7, 10, 11, 19, 22–24, 28, 33, 35–37, 39 & 40: Royal Commission on the Historical Monuments of England
Plates 4, 5, 15–18, 20, 38, 41–43, 45–50: English Heritage
Plate 1: Anthony Burnett-Brown
Plates 2, 21: Chapman Taylor Partners
Plate 3: The Architect's Department, Winchester City Council
Plate 8: Ruth Goodman
Plate 9: F. W. B. Charles
Plates 12–13: J. H. Benson, R. A. Maguire and P. Matthews
Plate 14: R. S. Fitzgerald, Curator, Industrial Archaeology, Leeds Industrial Museum
Plates 25–27: Mrs E. Cartwright, Hignett and the Northamptonshire Record Office
Plates 29–32: Sir John Cotterell, Bart.
Plate 34: Caroe and Martin (survey by Henk Strik on behalf of the Landmark Trust)
Plate 44: The Dean and Chapter of Lichfield Cathedral (survey by AMC Surveyors under the direction of Martin Stancliffe)

INTRODUCTION
PURPOSES OF RECORDING

Historic buildings are irreplaceable, and contain information about the past that is available from no other source. They must be treated responsibly, and the understanding that is essential to their proper treatment can only be reached by making use of the best possible information about them and by ensuring too that future generations understand what the present generation has done for their care. The purpose of recording is to make the interpretation of a historic building available when and where it may be needed, while the purpose of this book is to discuss why and when buildings ought to be recorded, the techniques that exist for doing it, who may be the best people to undertake it, and the actual procedures that may conveniently be followed (Figure 1).

There are two stages to recording. The first is to establish and to illustrate the historical significance of the building and of its details, so that those concerned with it (owners, administrators, architects, surveyors, planners and historians) may be fully aware of the historical importance of the building and of its parts. This entails recording the building before undertaking – or even specifying – any work that may have to be done to it; it also involves keeping a close watch for relevant information that may appear in the course of work and, as a corollary to that, being prepared so far as possible to alter one's intentions in the light of new information. The second stage is to record whatever work is actually carried out. The record of a building should thus be seen as cumulative, with each stage adding both to the comprehensiveness of the record and to the comprehension of the building that the record makes possible.

There is no one way to record buildings that is ideal in all circumstances, but the end should always be the same: to heighten the understanding of a building's use and history, to show why it is like it is and what has been done to it, and to indicate its historical importance, its significant structural and decorative features, and the elements that it is essential to preserve. The phrase 'analytical recording' is sometimes used in connection with this process of appraisal. This is discussed rather more fully in Chapter 4. But while this analysis is fundamental to the recording process (since without it one does not know what to record), it must nearly always be supplemented by graphic and visual records as well – by photography, and by survey drawing produced by whatever techniques are appropriate to the job in hand. A book of this size cannot be a manual of instruction, but these techniques are also discussed further in Chapter 4. Chapter 1 discusses why recording is important, and the uses that can be made of records by the various people who may be concerned with a building. Chapter 2 discusses the circumstances in which a record should be made. Chapter 3 discusses the process of selection: the recognition of significant features and the extent of new work that will call for recording. Chapters 5 and 6 concern who should make the record, how and where records should be kept, and the practical procedures that they might follow.

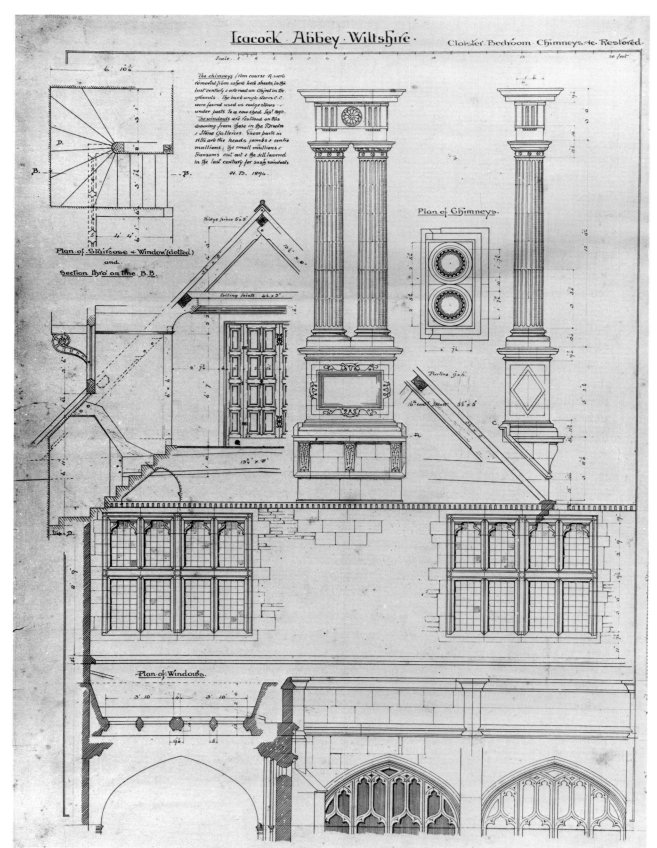

Figure 1 Lacock Abbey, Wiltshire; elevational details, as recorded in 1894

CHAPTER 1

WHY?

OBJECTIVES OF RECORDING

The first object of a survey should be to record what is necessary in order to understand and to illustrate the history of the building, its plan, structure, development, use and decoration (Figure 2). Records should be made of such features to inform the architect's own decisions, which in turn he sets out in drawings and specifications that will inform a contractor of those elements that are to be preserved, restored or accurately reproduced. Similarly, architects and contractors in the future will want to know what has been done here and now, and, if the work has involved structural repair, the reasons why it had to be done. On occasions, too, when specialist conservation treatment is called for, a record should be made of the object to be conserved before work starts, so that the conservator has a base for reference and so that in the future, if any further treatment is needed, the original form and condition of the object are known, together with the circumstances that made such treatment necessary.

Records of buildings are needed by their owners. In the last resort it is the owner of a building who is responsible for what is done to it, and he needs to understand it as much as his architect does, even though he may lack the technical knowledge to read an architect's drawing or to understand a specification. Much that an owner may do, in any case, may be done without professional advice or assistance. Besides, most people have some curiosity about the history of the house they live in, and they will probably look after it better if they know something about it. Future owners of a building will find a full record, adequately illustrated with drawings and photographs, an invaluable guide not only to planned restoration but in case of fire or other accident. The aim should be to build up a comprehensive logbook of the treatment of the building over the years, including recording where additional information not contained in the logbook itself can be found.

A record of the significant historical facts about a building is important to the administrator and the planner, so that they can base planning and other decisions on accurate information about it and so that they can produce evidence in support of these decisions (Figure 3). An obvious example is that of the planning officer who uses the list description of a building in considering an application for listed building consent: the description is a record, to be used as an administrative tool, but more detailed information – a fuller record – both of what the building is and of what is proposed is often needed before the implications for the building can be properly assessed. Grant applications are another obvious area where accurate records are needed as supporting evidence. Planning authorities need, in addition, to know the historic and environmental resources of their district, so that they can take these into account in framing local and strategic plans and in considering how to develop amenities.

Building records are needed as a management tool by those who have the care of a building,

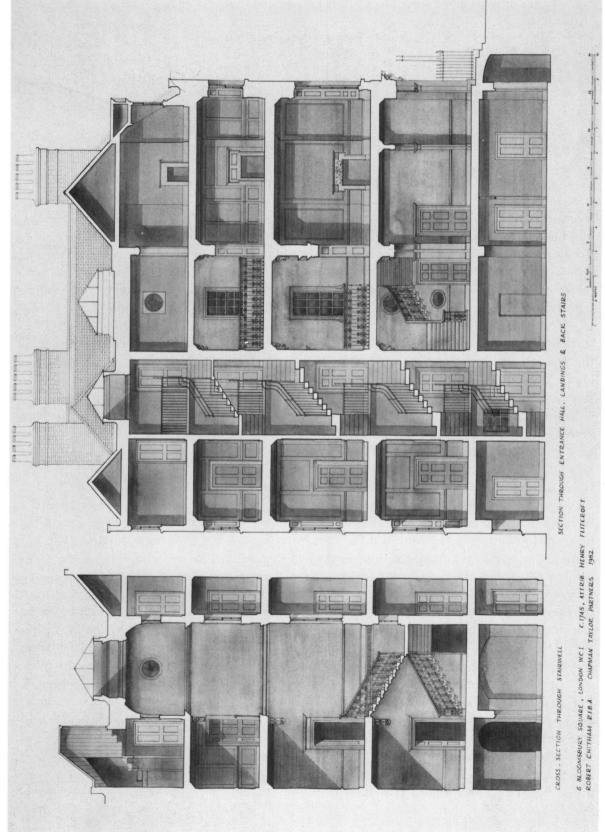

CROSS SECTION THROUGH STAIRWELL

SECTION THROUGH ENTRANCE HALL, LANDINGS & BACK STAIRS

6 BLOOMSBURY SQUARE, LONDON WC1 C.1745, ATTRIB HENRY FLITCROFT
ROBERT CHITHAM RIBA CHAPMAN TAYLOR PARTNERS 1982

Figure 2 6 Bloomsbury Square, London WC1; sections through the principal rooms and staircases

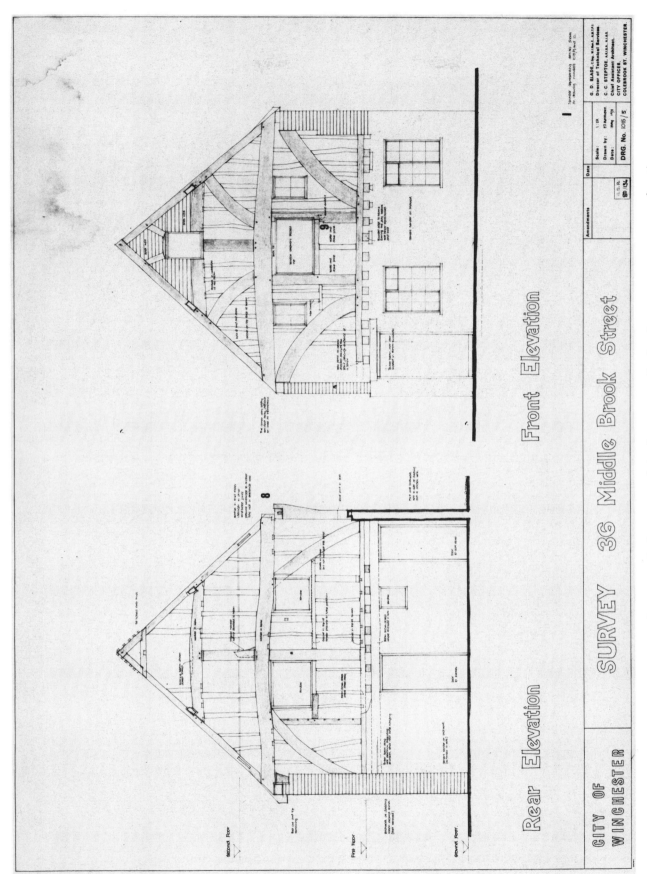

Figure 3 36 Middle Brook Street, Winchester; recorded prior to an application for consents to carry out alterations

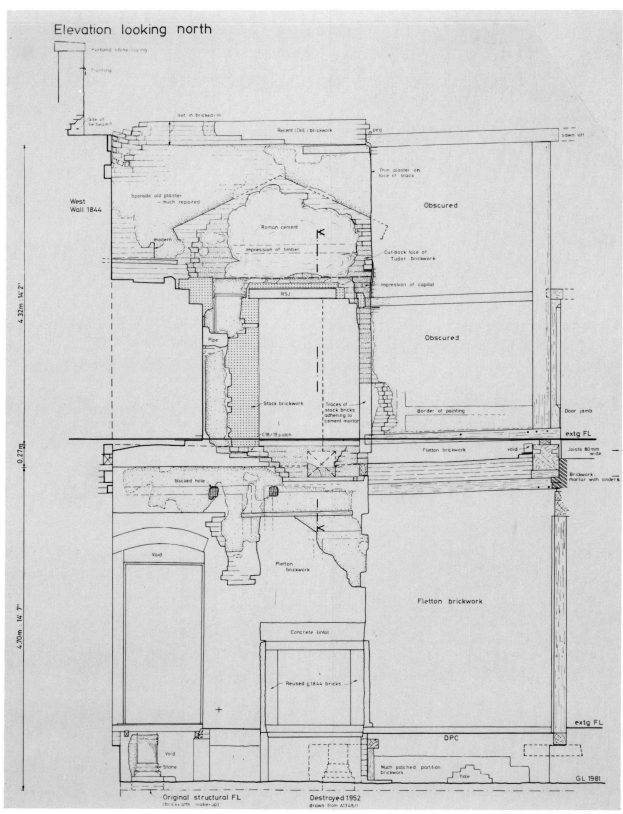

Figure 4   Hill Hall, Epping, Essex; part of internal elevation, showing different materials and identifying recent repairs. Part of the process of analysis necessary for planning further repair work

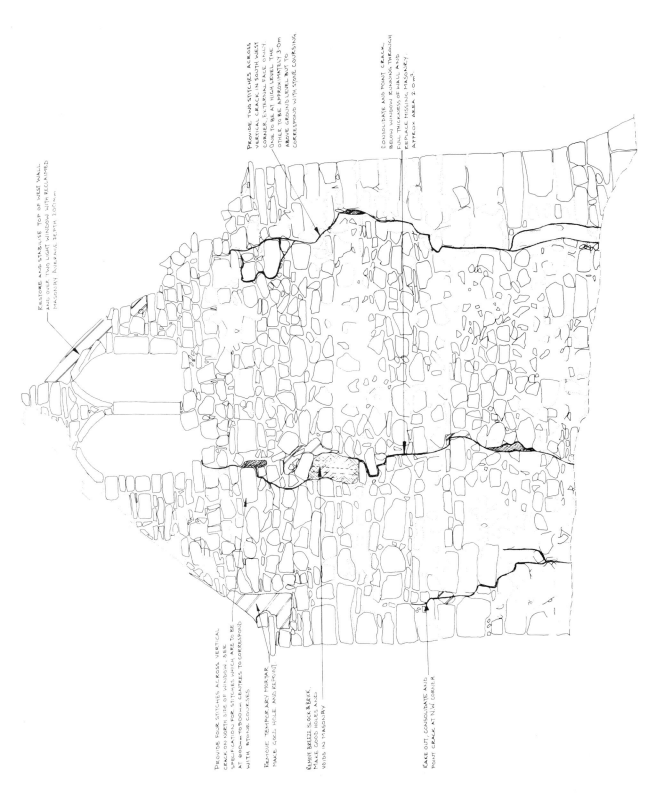

RESTORE AND STABILISE TOP OF WEST WALL AND OVER TWO LIGHT WINDOW WITH RECLAIMED MASONRY. AVERAGE DEPTH 200mm

PROVIDE TWO STITCHES ACROSS VERTICAL CRACK IN SOUTH WEST CORNER. EXTERNAL FACE ONLY. ONE TO BE AT HIGH LEVEL. THE OTHER TO BE APPROXIMATELY 3·0m ABOVE GROUND LEVEL, BUT TO CORRESPOND WITH STONE COURSING.

CONSOLIDATE AND POINT CRACK BELOW WINDOW RUNNING THROUGH FULL THICKNESS OF WALL AND REPLACE MISSING MASONRY. APPROX AREA 2·0 m².

PROVIDE FOUR STITCHES ACROSS VERTICAL CRACK ON NORTH SIDE OF WINDOW. SEE SPECIFICATION FOR STITCHES WHICH ARE TO BE AT 600mm TO 800mm CENTRES TO CORRESPOND WITH STONE COURSES.

REMOVE TEMPORARY MORTAR. MAKE GOOD HOLE AND REPOINT

REMOVE BREEZE BLOCK & BRICK. MAKE GOOD HOLES AND VOIDS IN MASONRY

RAKE OUT, CONSOLIDATE AND POINT CRACK AT N.W. CORNER

Figure 5 St James's Church, Lancaut, Gloucestershire; elevation of gable wall showing structural defects and indicating a schedule of repair

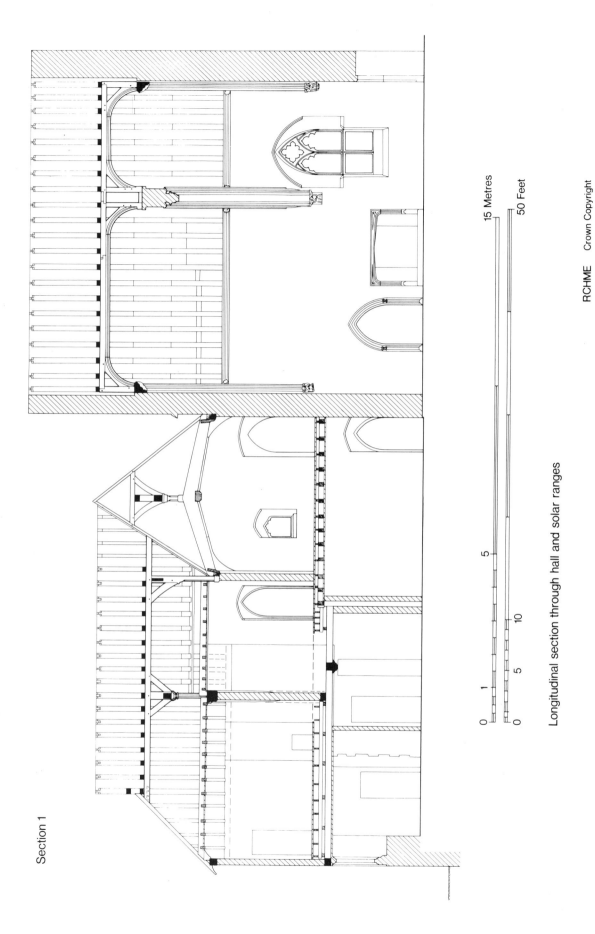

Section 1

Longitudinal section through hall and solar ranges

RCHME   Crown Copyright

0   1
0   5   10
0   5   15 Metres
     50 Feet

Figure 6   Ightham Mote, Kent; section through the hall and solars. The building is substantially of one build, but altered in the ground floor of the solar range and with an inserted fireplace in the hall. The section well explains the complexity of the arrangement of the building

even when no major work is being carried out to the structure (Figure 4). Surveyors need records in assessing the condition and potential of the buildings they are called upon to appraise. Knowledge of the building's structural history makes it easier to come to an accurate assessment of its present state and to recognize any structural faults (Figure 5). Records are needed in planning a maintenance programme, in monitoring the long-term effects of repair and remedial works, in identifying defects that may appear over time, in deciding whether any historical aspects of the building call for specially careful treatment (e.g. areas of historic decoration, or where historic construction may not safely meet modern loading requirements), or in assessing whether any historic features of it deserve exploitation (e.g. by showing the building to the public).

The final group of people who need records are historians. Historians need records of buildings to show how people lived and worked in the past, as well as how they designed and built. Buildings can throw light on many broad historical questions – questions about economic, religious and social conditions, about the spread of ideas, and about how such conditions change over time (Figure 6). To answer such questions, historians need to understand buildings as they were, rather than as restorations have made them; they need accurate and authentic information about how a building was built, used and altered. Historians want to know about the past as it really was, and buildings are among the most eloquent artefacts that have come down to us from the past. Records of buildings facilitate the historian's work, and by the use of records the historian can feed information about what is important in a building back to the architects and the administrator who may have neither the time nor the expertise to acquire such information for themselves.

CHAPTER 2

WHEN?

OCCASIONS FOR RECORDING

Records should be made whenever the people mentioned in Chapter 1 have a use for them. These people's needs will generally arise in connection with certain categories of buildings:

● Historically complex buildings that call for a particularly well-informed understanding of them if they are to be treated sympathetically (Figure 7). Such buildings may not necessarily be large ones; on the other hand, the fact that a building is large and well known is no guarantee that it is either properly recorded or well understood. The reverse is often the case.

● Buildings that are good examples of a particular type, form or style. These may be large and well known (Figure 8), or small and apparently insignificant but still of historical importance as illustrating living conditions at the level of the common man (Figure 9).

● Buildings that pose or answer historical problems, irrespective of their architectural merits (Figures 10 and 11). Some apparently ordinary structures (e.g. farm buildings and industrial structures) throw much light on the economy that produced them and on the daily life of the past.

● Buildings containing innovations of structure or design (Figures 12–14).

● Buildings that call for authenticity for non-architectural reasons (e.g. the places associated with great events or people, and which need to be preserved as they were at a particular time).

● All buildings where work is to be carried out and the owner, his architect or his surveyor want to know about the history and structural condition of the building before work begins.

● All buildings where work is being carried out and there is a reasonable expectation that people in the future may want to know what is being done now, and how (Figures 15–17).

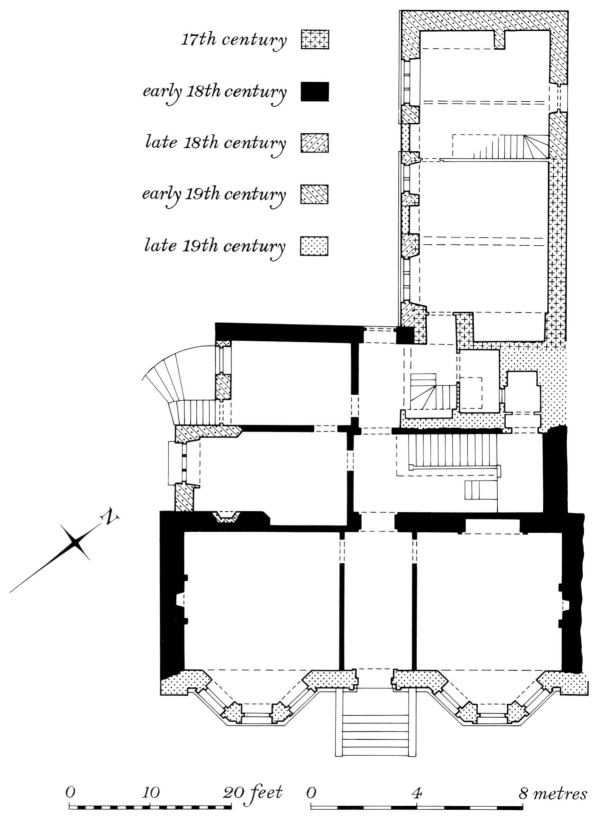

17th century

early 18th century

late 18th century

early 19th century

late 19th century

0   10   20 feet   0   4   8 metres

Figure 7   Broad Street, Stamford, Lincolnshire; ground floor plan. A good example of the indication of the dates and sequence of different building phases. Where the building history is very complicated, such a plan may need to be augmented by analytical elevations and sections and other material, and in any case the drawn record should be accompanied by a written account setting out the reasons for the conclusions reached

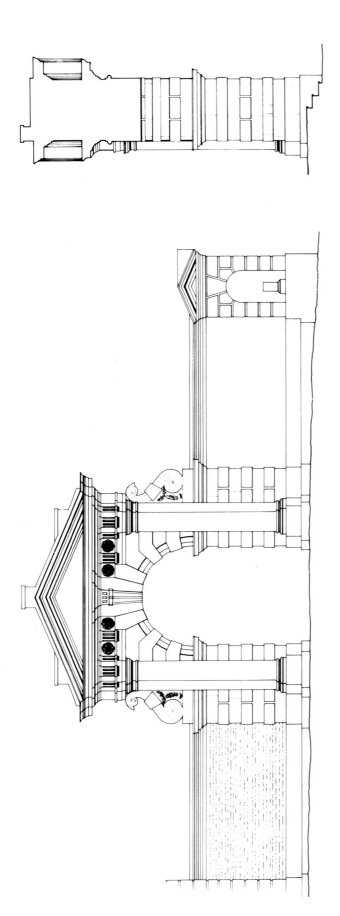

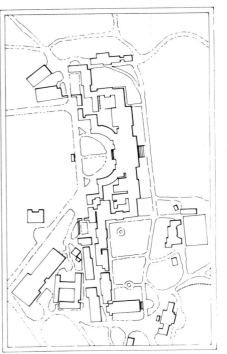

Figure 8 Stowe, Buckinghamshire; screen and archway at the east side of the entrance front. An example of the designs of Giacomo Leoni, *c.* 1740

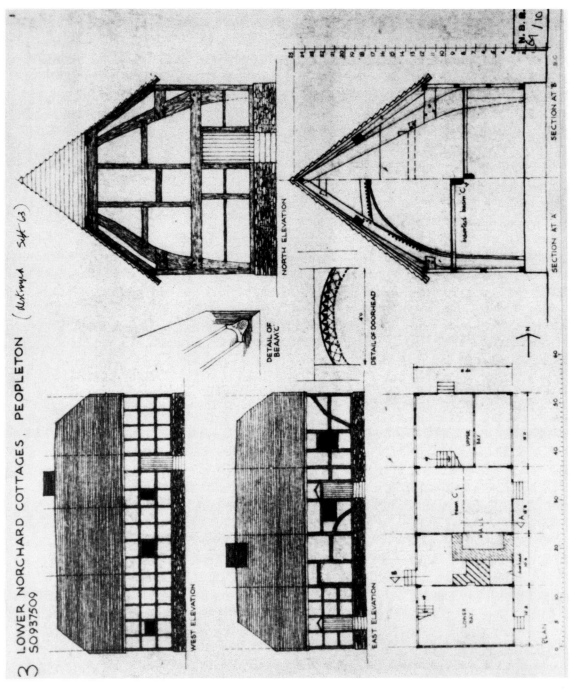

Figure 9 Lower Norchard Cottages, Peopleton, Worcestershire; plan, section and elevation. One of a series of drawings recording the layout and construction of medieval vernacular housing in the district

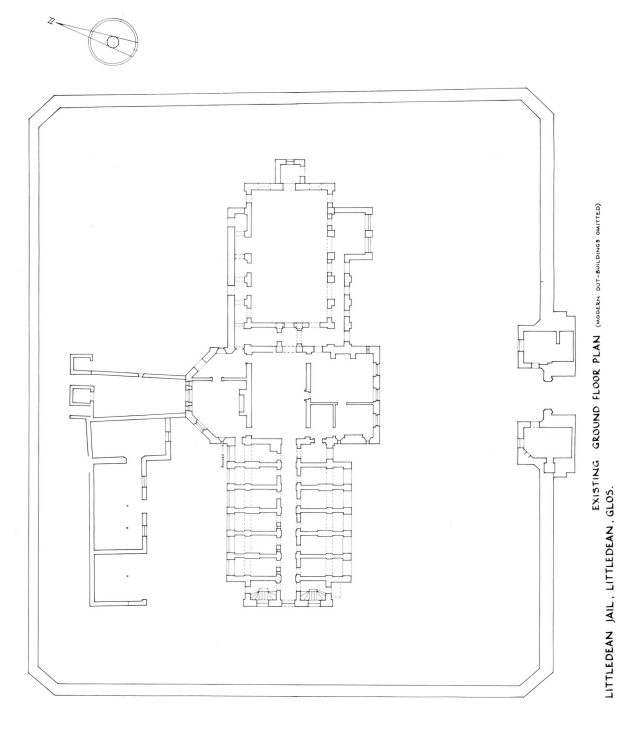

N

EXISTING GROUND FLOOR PLAN (MODERN OUT-BUILDINGS OMITTED)

LITTLEDEAN JAIL, LITTLEDEAN, GLOS.

R.C.H.M.E. 1988

Figure 10 Littledean Jail, Gloucestershire; this figure shows the existing plan, Figure 11 the late eighteenth century plan reconstructed, giving an insight into the form and arrangement of a penal institution towards the end of the century, and showing its subsequent adaptation

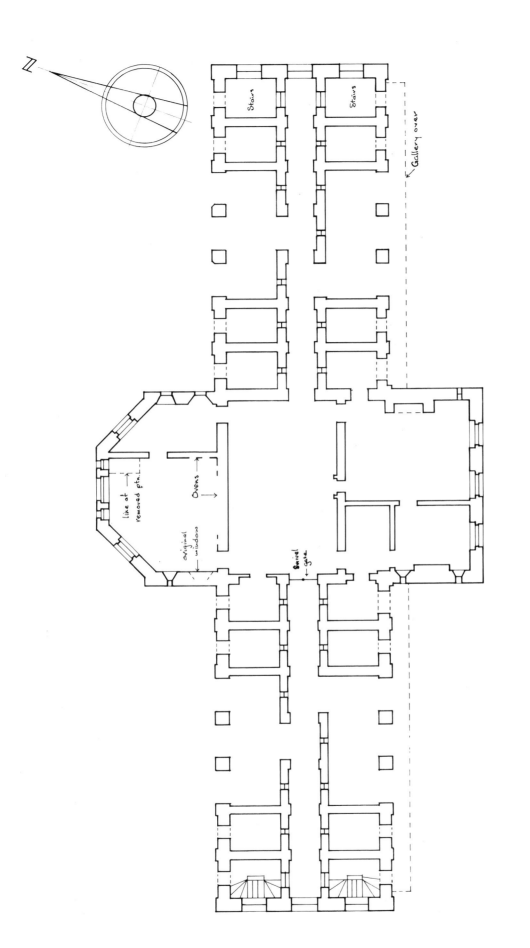

GROUND FLOOR PLAN

LITTLEDEAN JAIL, LITTLEDEAN, GLOS.

RCHME.   1988.

Figure 11   See Figure 10

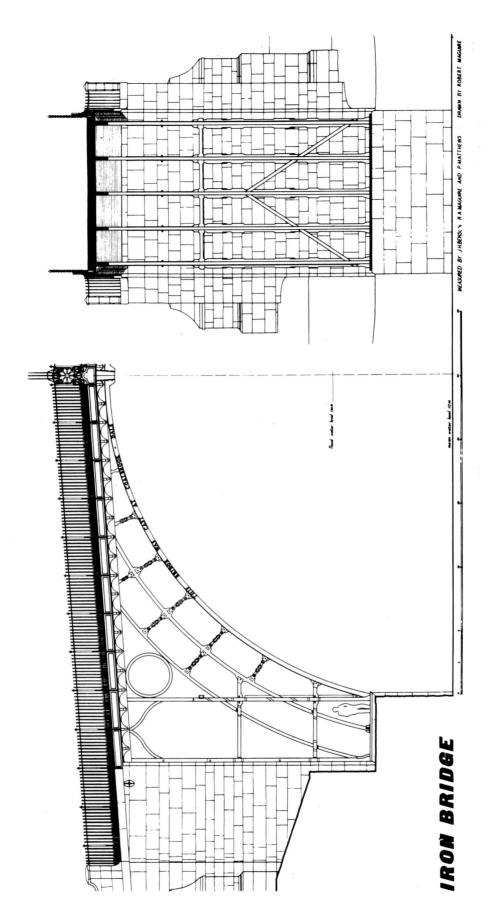

IRON BRIDGE

MEASURED BY J HIBENS V R A MAGUIRE AND P MATTHEWS   DRAWN BY ROBERT MAGUIRE

Figure 12 The Iron Bridge, Ironbridge, Shropshire; half-elevation, section and (Figure 13) details of components. Record drawings of the earliest cast iron bridge manufactured by Abraham Darby at Coalbrookdale in 1778

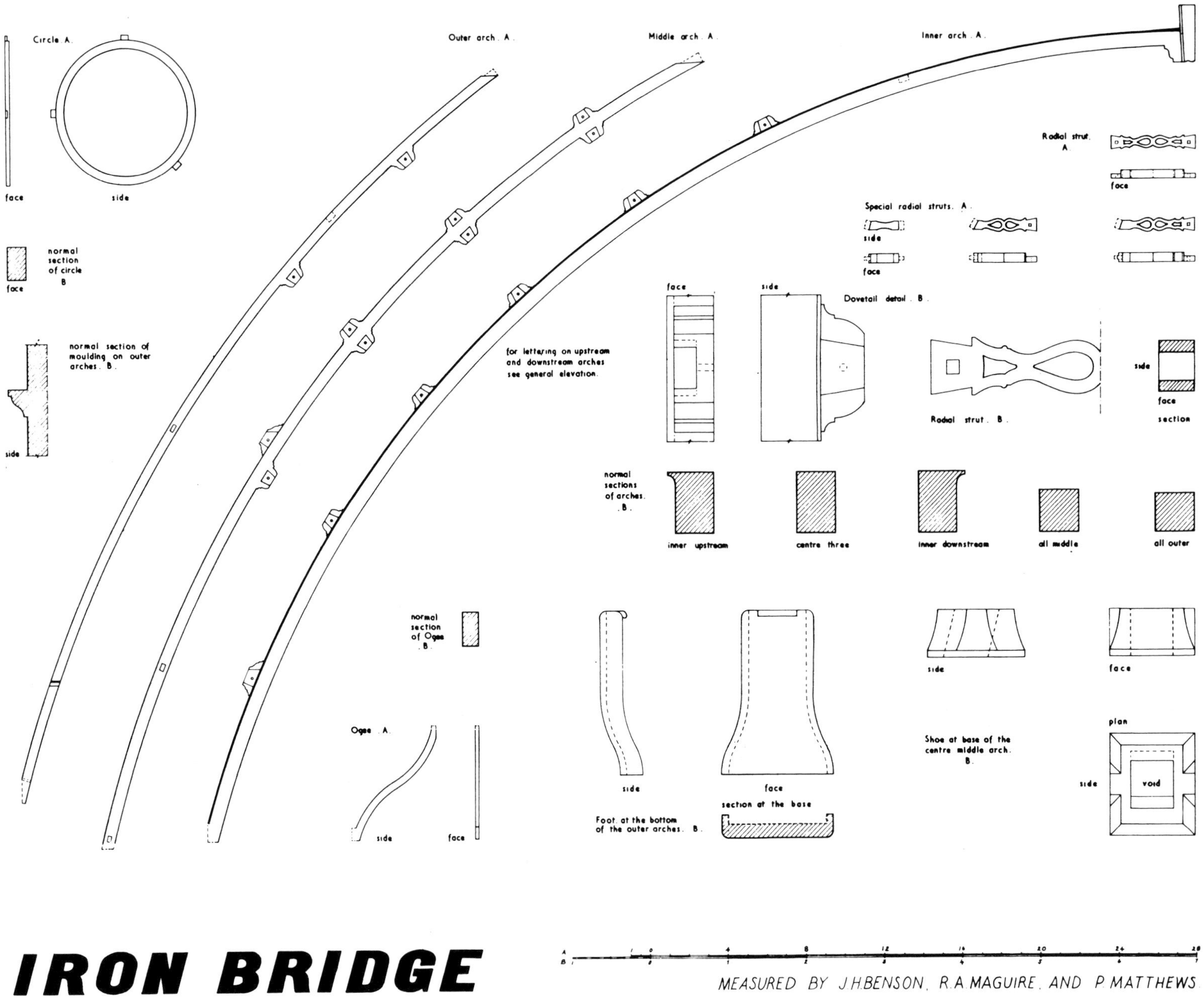

IRON BRIDGE

Inner arch. A.

Middle arch. A.

Outer arch. A.

Circle A.

side

face

normal section of circle B

face

normal section of moulding on outer arches. B

side

Radial strut. A.

face

Special radial struts. A.

side

Radial strut B

Dovetail detail B

side

face

side

face

(for lettering on upstream and downstream arches see general elevation.)

side

face

normal section of Ogee B

Ogee. A.

face

side

face

section

all outer

all middle

inner downstream

centre three

inner upstream

normal sections of arches. B.

face

side

face

side

Shoe at base of the centre middle arch. B.

plan

void

side

face

section of the base

side

Foot at the bottom of the outer arches. B.

MEASURED BY J.H.BENSON, R.A.MAGUIRE, AND P.MATTHEWS

Figure 13   See Figure 12

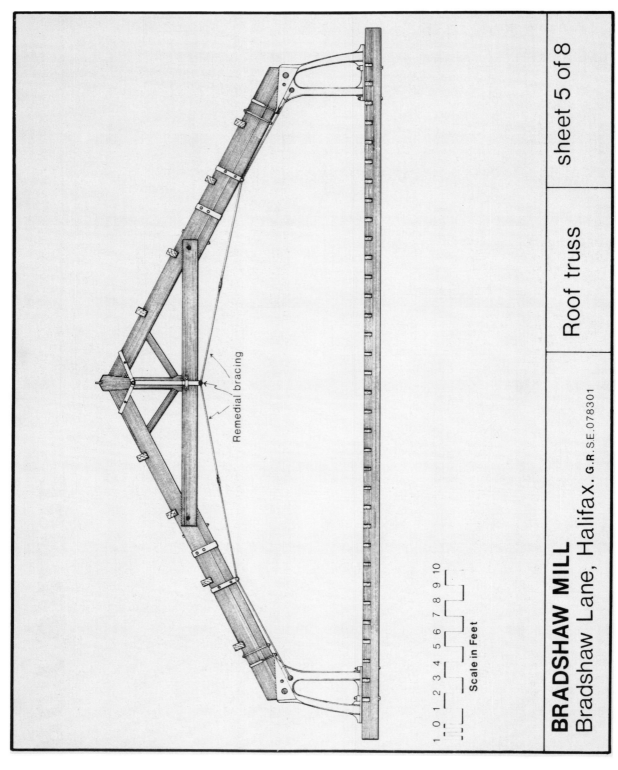

Remedial bracing

1 0 1 2 3 4 5 6 7 8 9 10
Scale in Feet

BRADSHAW MILL
Bradshaw Lane, Halifax. **G.R.** SE.078301

Roof truss

sheet 5 of 8

Figure 14 Bradshaw Mill, Halifax, Yorkshire; elevation of roof truss. An elaborate and innovative nineteenth century method of attaining a considerable span using a compound timber and iron structure. The tensile bracing shown as remedial may be part of the original design

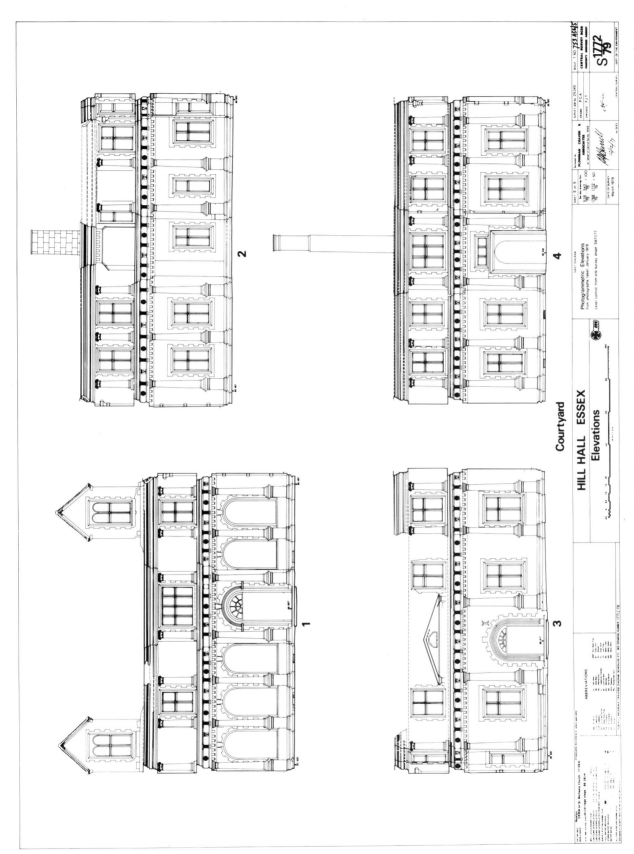

Courtyard

HILL HALL ESSEX

Elevations

Figure 15 Hill Hall, Epping, Essex; photogrammetric survey of part of the courtyard elevation before the inception of work. See also Figures 16 and 17

Figure 16 Hill Hall, Epping, Essex; progress photograph showing details revealed by the removal of later material. See also Figures 15 and 17

Recording is almost always important, but is is more important in some circumstances than in others. The particular circumstances of each building will in some degree affect the matter to be recorded, but occasions that will almost always give rise to the need for a record age are:

• work involving the total or partial demolition of structures of historical, architectural or engineering interest;

• work involving the destruction or concealment of any evidence for the building's origin and development;

• work involving the destruction of historical decoration;

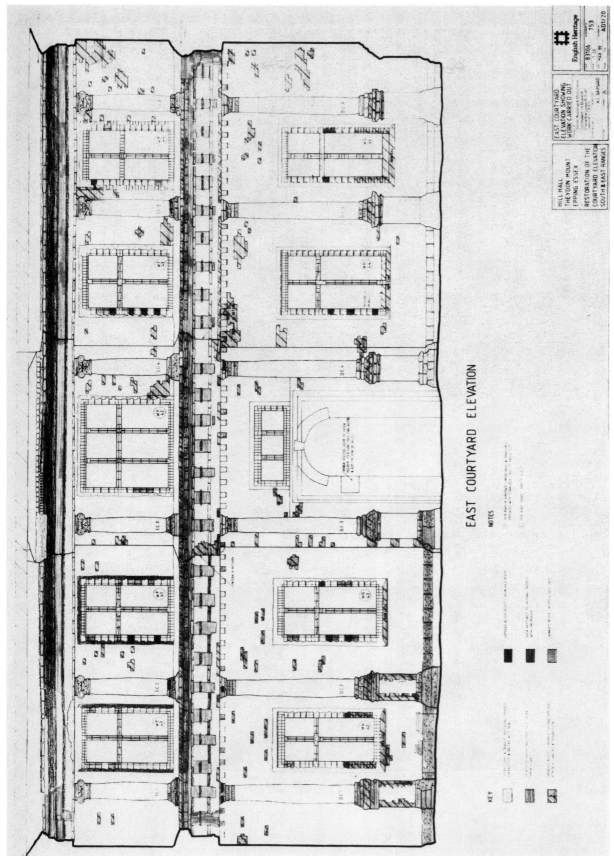

EAST COURTYARD ELEVATION

Figure 17 Hill Hall, Epping, Essex; survey drawing annotated to show the extent of work carried out, as well as the details of earlier interventions. See also Figures 15 and 16

Figure 18   Hill Hall, Epping, Essex; part of the ground floor, south range. Excavation of the base of the stair (left) revealed the footings of an earlier stair-tower wall; traces of the abutment of this wall are also visible on the inner face of the external wall (right)

Figure 19 The Archbishop's Palace, Maidstone, Kent; a further example of evidence of earlier structures revealed by removal of wall coverings and excavation of the floor – in this case a sixteenth century fireplace as well as the footings and abutment of a medieval wall

- work involving the destruction of fittings, plant, etc., essential to the building's structure, purpose or design;

- major repairs of all kinds;

- work involving the temporary exposure, in the course of repair, of historical evidence normally concealed;

- work involving remedial treatment that may call for monitoring over time;

- work involving the insertion of services, etc., whose location must be recorded;

- fires or other accidental damage;

- abandonment of the building, accepting its subsequent deterioration;

- work of stone-cleaning, as well as instances of severe masonry deterioration where the danger of loss of detail may result;

- dispersal of contents

and in all cases when, as outlined already, a proper comprehension of the building is important to its proper treatment.

It is important to realize that even though work may affect only one part of a building, it may be necessary to record other areas in order to reach an understanding of it. It will be obvious that one can only tell if a part of a building is original or secondary by looking at the rest of it. Additions may be inexplicable without comparison with what they were added to. Elsewhere, evidence in one part will throw light on work in another. For instance, if one roof truss needs repair, evidence for its original form may be found at the other end of the roof, or if mouldings are badly eroded, evidence for their original form may have to be sought in another part of the building. In addition to initial recording, it will often be necessary to return to the site periodically during demolition or radical alteration, to record information brought to light by the works.

Evidence for a building's history may lie below ground as well as above it, and when this is suspected of being the case (as with most buildings of which only a part now stands, or buildings that stand on sites where earlier occupation is suspected), then the below-ground evidence should be investigated at the same time as that above ground (Figures 18 and 19). Other occasions when this should be done are when excavation for services may disturb remains associated with the building – remains such as foundations, burials, traces of garden layouts, etc.

Recording may be required as a condition of listed building consent or as a condition of repair grant from a local planning authority or from English Heritage. Archaeological recording below ground is often a condition of scheduled monument consent, and is sometimes called for in other cases. Full use should be made of the information and expertise that may be available through the involvement of organizations such as English Heritage and the Royal Commission on Historical Monuments, and through regional Archaeological Units (see Chapter 5).

CHAPTER 3

WHAT?

FEATURES THAT REQUIRE RECORDING

As a preliminary to recording, it is important to discover what records exist already. These may reduce or eliminate the need for further recording; they may contain information that throws light on the building's history and explain features otherwise inexplicable. Such records are of many kinds and available from many different sources; this is discussed further in Chapter 4.

The features that require recording are a mixture of evidence and conclusions: facts about a building's structure, form and decoration and the conclusions about the building's history that have been derived from this evidence. The building recorder identifies his evidence, and comes to conclusions about how the building was built and used. The administrator needs the recorder's appraisal of the building, and may in addition want a record of the evidence for his conclusions. The architect needs these conclusions also, and should understand the evidence for them so that it can be physically preserved in the building. He needs, too, to know the nature of the evidence and to understand its strength, in case further information comes to light in the course of work that may lead to a modification of the original interpretation. In addition, the surveyor and engineer need facts of their own – facts about the building's structural system and condition, about services and about previous work. Some of these will be items of which everyone involved will want a record; others may be of limited general concern but none the less give rise to conclusions about the building that are of value to everybody.

Items that will generally call for record include:

- overall form and dimensions – evidence for the original form of the building and for its evolution over time (Figures 20 and 21);

- materials and construction – type of foundations, wall structure, roof (Figure 22);

- decoration and ornament (Figures 23 and 24);

- plant and fittings;

- evidence for the use of the building and for changes in its use over time;

- dating evidence – this may be absolute or relative.

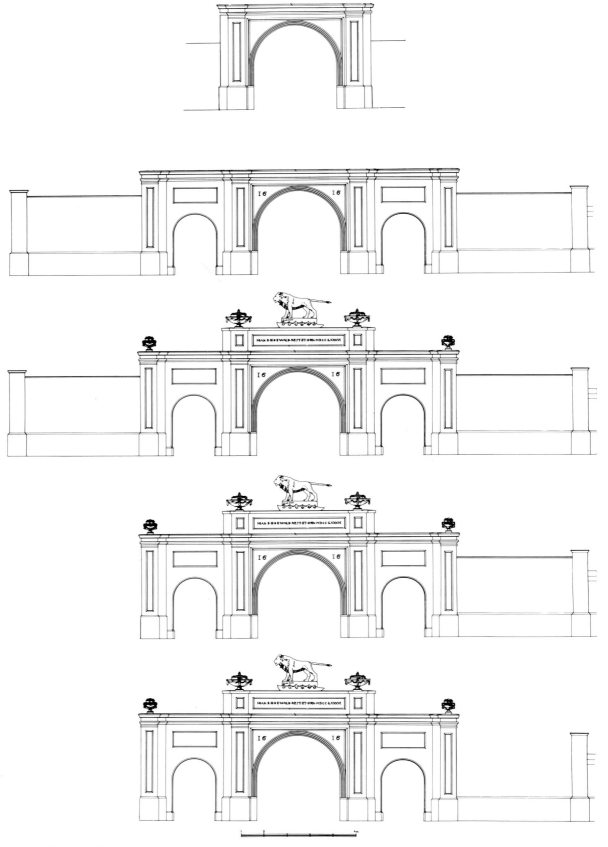

Figure 20   Audley End, Essex; a series of elevations of the Lion Gate, compiled from measurement and the study of existing records, showing its evolution from the earliest to the present form

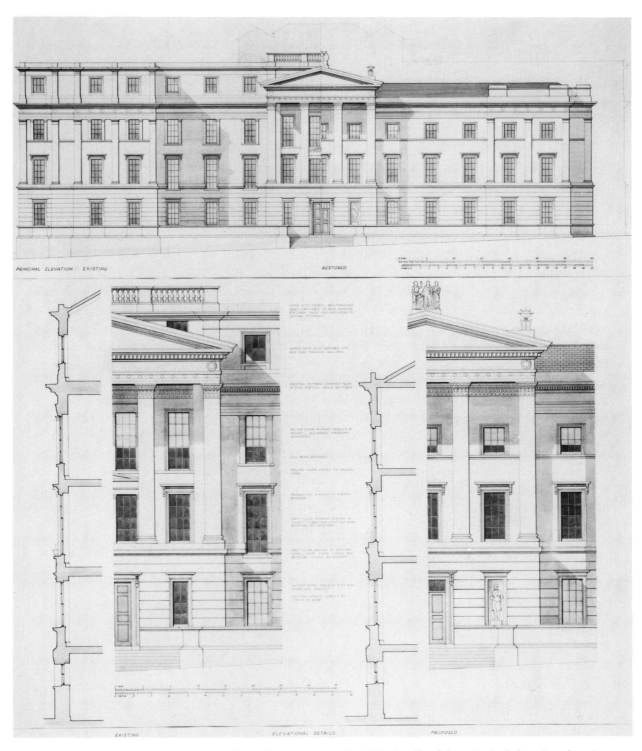

PRINCIPAL ELEVATION : EXISTING   RESTORED

EXISTING   ELEVATIONAL DETAILS   PROPOSED

Figure 21   St. George's Hospital, Hyde Park Corner, London W1; details of the principal elevation showing its state in 1980 and the conjectural restoration of its original form, from a combination of site measurement and investigation, rectified photography and documentary research

Figure 22 Purton Green Farm, Stansfield, Suffolk; appearance of an early roof with passing braces, recorded photographically

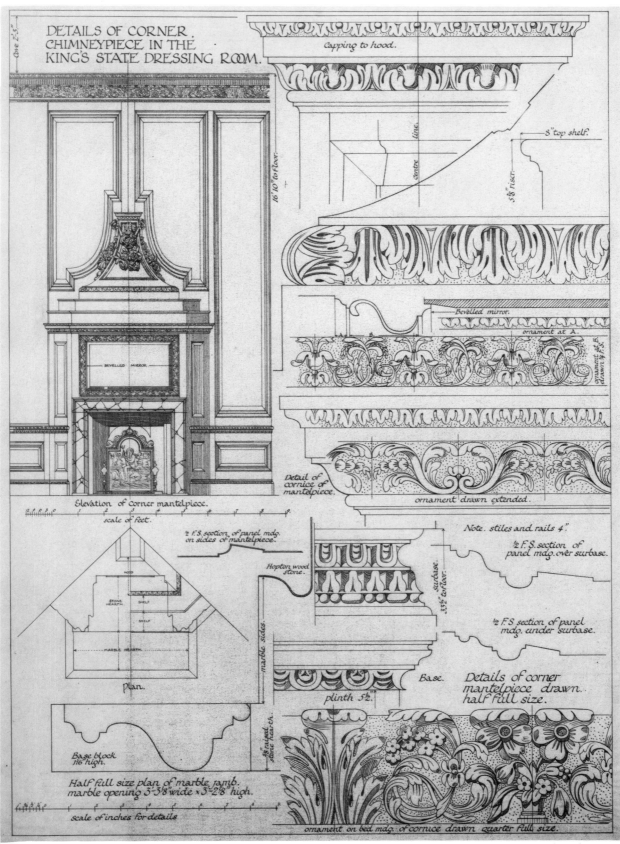

DETAILS OF CORNER.
CHIMNEYPIECE IN THE
KING'S STATE DRESSING ROOM.

Capping to hood.

8" top shelf.

Bevelled mirror.

ornament at A.

ornament at B. drawn ½ F.S.

Detail of cornice of mantelpiece.

ornament drawn extended.

Elevation of corner mantelpiece.

scale of feet.

½ F.S. section of panel mdg. on sides of mantelpiece.

Note. stiles and rails 4".

½ F.S. section of panel mdg. over surbase.

Hopton wood stone.

½ F.S section of panel mdg. under surbase.

HOOD

STONE HEARTH

SHELF

SHELF

MARBLE HEARTH

marble sides

plan.

Base.

Details of corner mantelpiece drawn. half full size.

plinth 5½.

Base block 1½ high.

Half full size plan of marble jamb. marble opening 3'-5⅜" wide × 3'-2⅜" high.

scale of inches for details

ornament on bed mdg. of cornice drawn quarter full size.

Figure 23 Hampton Court Palace; decorative details. The drawings here and in Figure 24, executed in the early part of the century, are among a series which was of great value in carrying out the major restoration following the recent fire

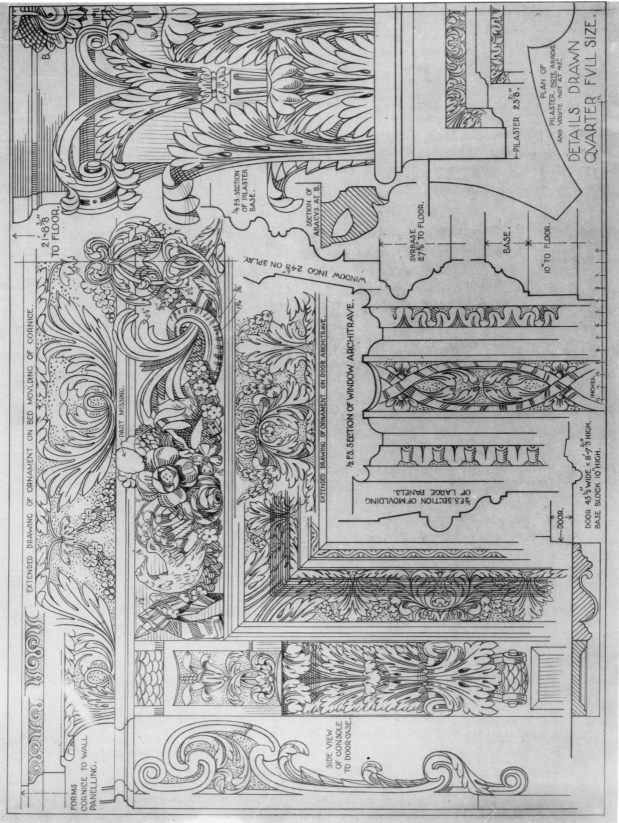

Figure 24　See Figure 23

Recording should also include information about ancillary buildings, garden and estate layouts, and enclosures, and the relationship with adjoining buildings especially where this is of a formal nature. In addition, notes should be made of items on the site which are clearly not in their current location.

Some of these enquiries may be answered by looking at documents, even though the implications of documents should always be checked against the evidence of the building itself before they are accepted as a true and accurate account of what may have happened. In many other cases, it may be possible to reach conclusions on some of these points only after careful and minute examination of the fabric of the building. In Appendix I is a list of the evidence that may be looked for, and recorded where appropriate, in support of these conclusions; Chapter 4 discusses how this evidence can be used.

The foregoing list should be used at the outset, in considering proposals. It should also be borne in mind during the progress of the work: frequently in stripping-out or in the course of further work, evidence will come to light that bears on all these issues. Any such discoveries should be recorded: they may have a bearing on the interpretation of the building, may demand a reappraisal of a scheme for the building's treatment, and will in any case be important to the historian since they may modify his original view of it.

Particular attention should be paid to recording any work in these categories that is to be covered up or destroyed. While some evidence that remains clearly visible and untouched may call for no more than a note, anything that is to be lost must be recorded fully and unambiguously so that there can be as little doubt as possible about its interpretation. There will, however, always be elements in a building that cannot be understood, and these also should be recorded in case subsequent discoveries may serve to explain them.

There are occasions when material samples may be subjected to scientific analysis to determine their composition (such as a mortar make-up, a stone type, or the materials used in an earlier conservation programme), their structural properties or physical condition, or their date. Expert guidance should always be sought in these fields, and reports of experts' findings carefully preserved.

CHAPTER 4

HOW?
APPROACHES AND TECHNIQUES

As a first step, it is important to look for any documentary material that may throw light on the building's history or condition. There are many kinds of such material, and it may be sought in many different places. It will nearly always be found that the following are useful:

- *Survey and architectural drawings*. The accuracy of existing drawings must never be assumed; none the less they are obviously of the greatest value, particularly when they show work to be carried out or an earlier stage in a building's development.

- *Written descriptions* (published or unpublished). Where these are the result of a first-hand examination of the fabric or of documents relating to it (e.g. accounts, specifications, diaries) they can be of great value; on the other hand, there is a tendency, particularly in the published descriptions of well-known buildings, for historical statements to be repeated uncritically from earlier writers, and old accounts are often less reliable than modern ones.

- *Other documents*. These can be of many sorts – diaries, letters, or building accounts and vouchers. They may relate to the building's origin or to its later history. The interpretation of these sources, particularly when they are old, may require specialist help: terms may be obscure, handwriting may be difficult to decipher, the arrangement of information in accounts may seem illogical, and the circumstances of their making must be understood in order to comprehend both the potential of such documents and the limits on what to expect from them.

- *Old illustrations*. Sketches, paintings and prints can be dangerously subjective (Figures 25–28). Moreover, if a drawing or an engraving has been made not from the building itself but by copying an existing illustration of it, misrepresentation may appear as truth simply because of the number of different images in which the misrepresentation occurs. But used with caution, such illustrations can be of great value (Figures 29–32). Photographs on the other hand are generally objective, and should always be looked for; they may very often be the only source of information available on relatively humble and little known buildings.

The range of potential sources for documentary information is huge, but in practice a point of diminishing returns will be recognized: after the more likely sources have been explored, it will seem increasingly improbable that the more obscure sources can help and the time spent in searching them will seldom be worth while.

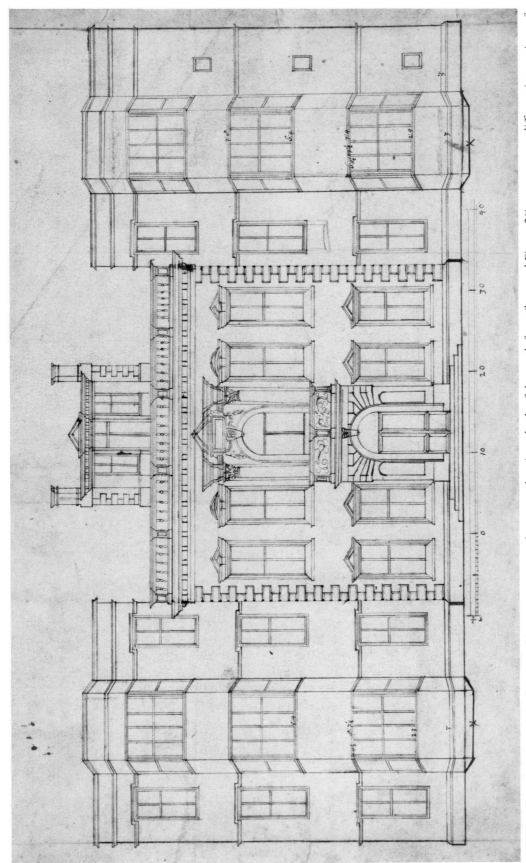

Figure 25 Aynho House, Northamptonshire; two seventeenth century drawings, both of the north front (here and Figure 26), convey very different impressions of the elevational details, e.g. the form and proportions of the bays in the wings, the pediment types to the windows in the centre, the relationship of the frontispiece with the crowning cornice, etc. See also Figures 27 and 28

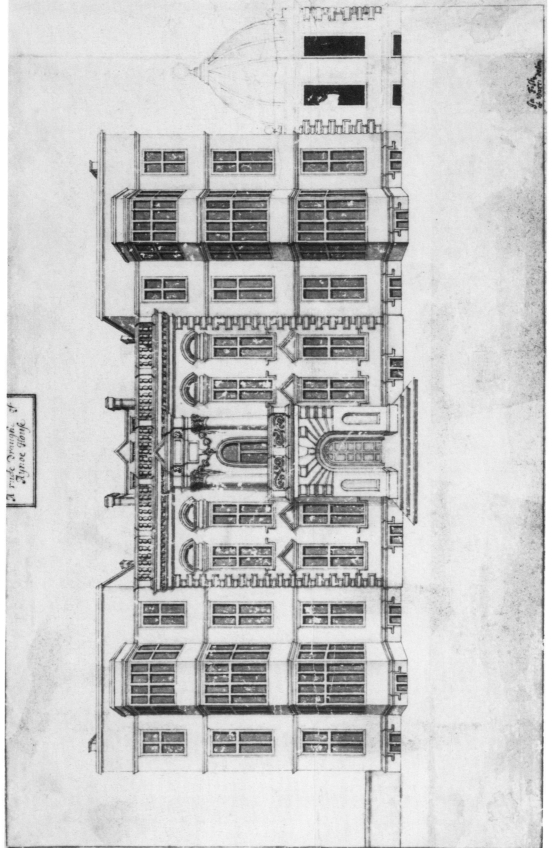

Figure 26 See Figure 25

Elevation of N°1. (with the Old Building) towards the South

Figure 27   Aynho House, Northamptonshire; Soane's drawing of the south front *c.* 1800 suggests that neither earlier drawing (Figures 25 and 26) was accurate, while the appearance of the north front today (Figure 28) is again different in detail

Figure 28 See Figure 27

Figure 29 Garnons, Herefordshire; a sequence of old illustrations (Figures 29–32) from which the history of the building can be charted with some accuracy. This topographical sketch of 1791 (by Repton) shows a proposal for the new house and its location

Figure 30 Garnons, Herefordshire; a view of the house about the time of its remodelling by William Atkinson in 1815–30

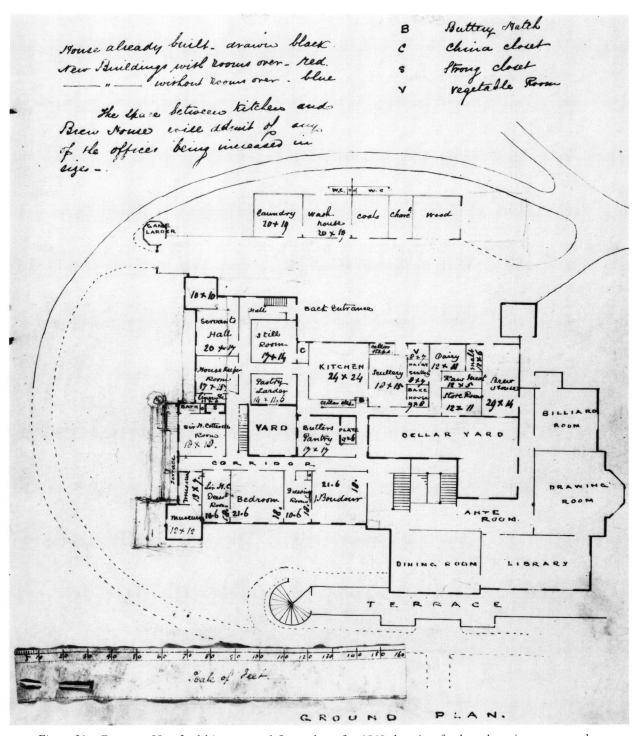

Figure 31   Garnons, Herefordshire; ground floor plan of *c.* 1860 showing further alterations proposed

Figure 32 Garnons, Herefordshire; a view – from the same aspect as Figure 30 – of the house *c.* 1870, the photography in this instance diminishing the picturesque nature of the surroundings

SOURCES OF INFORMATION – NATIONAL

The principal national sources are:

1. The lists of historic buildings produced by the Secretary of State for the Environment, 'The DoE Lists', and (for Scotland) the Secretary of State for Scotland. Some description is available in the lists for virtually all of the 500 000 or so listed buildings in England, Wales and Scotland. The information in these lists is of variable quality, depending on the date of survey and the qualifications of the surveyor, and in many cases was made from an external inspection only, ignoring historic features only visible from within. Listing in England is now carried out on the recommendation of the staff of English Heritage and in Wales by the staff of CADW (see Appendix II); in recent lists the account can be very full and of great value. These lists can be seen in some local libraries and planning offices, and all are available at the National Buildings Records (see below).

2. The National Buildings Records (NBRs). The English, Scottish and Welsh NBRs are the national public archives for photographs and for other unpublished records. These are run by the respective Royal Commissions on Historical Monuments (see below). Although most of the photographs held in the NBRs are of comparatively recent date, many go back to the last century, whereas the NBRs have since their establishment in the 1940s collected measured drawings and unpublished reports of all kinds.

3. Of published, national surveys of historic buildings, the volumes of *The Buildings of England* (Penguin Books) are well known and widely available. Each volume covers a county, providing a brief or a fuller description of the majority of the more significant buildings of England; the series is in progress for Scotland and Wales. A building described in this series may well be recorded more fully elsewhere.

   The articles in *Country Life* (from 1899 onwards, and increasingly full and accurate from the 1920s) are useful, although for the most part dealing only with country houses. Also valuable are the volumes of the *Royal Commissions on Historical Monuments* (for England, Scotland and Wales; the three Royal Commissions have slightly different titles). None of the three countries has been fully covered, but where coverage exists it is generally more detailed than that in the DoE lists. The original field notes, etc., from which the published accounts have been made are held in the respective NBRs (see above). Also useful, for London, are the volumes of the *Survey of London* (from 1896), which has covered about one-third of the Greater London area to date.

   The *Victoria County Histories* contain useful information about the more notable buildings of the places so far covered, being concerned in particular with the ownership and descent of such buildings; the series is complete for some counties, in progress for others, while in yet other counties work is in abeyance.

   All these sources (except *Country Life*) cover churches as well as houses and other secular buildings. For buildings erected since about 1840, it may be worth consulting the increasingly large range of professional journals, such as *The Builder* and *The Building News*. Most of these can be found in the public libraries of the major cities and in specialized libraries such as those of universities and of the RIBA in London.

SOURCES OF INFORMATION – LOCAL

The range of possible local sources is almost unlimited – previous owners, local historians and collections in local libraries, local architects who may have been concerned with the building, the archives of local newspapers, and so forth. Many of these will in practice prove difficult to locate without some prior knowledge (although there are many excellent guides to documentary sources published for the assistance of local historians), and possible sources of information may well prove unproductive. The most likely sources are:

1. *Published accounts,* often more readily available through the local history collections of the principal local public library. A great deal of local history (not all of it accurate, but much of it the result of research of a high standard) does not reach national publications. Useful information, particularly on older buildings, can be found in the transactions of national and local archaeological and historical societies, although the earlier volumes of some of these societies tend to contain information that reflects tradition rather than accurate first-hand analysis.
2. *Unpublished documents,* generally available through local (County) record offices. These exist for almost all counties and for some smaller and city authorities, and contain a mass of private and public documentary collections for the area they cover. There are generally very comprehensive indexes to the material and the collections held. Many County Record Offices also serve as Diocesan record offices for the area and thus contain church records as well as the records of the secular administration. The Church of England has its own statutory machinery for the deposition of parish records (the *Parochial Records Measure*), while most cathedral churches have an official archive and archivist.
3. *Local government offices.* The chief source here is likely to be Building Control plans and documents, and although the majority of these will be found to be site plans only, showing the location of services, others will show the detailed form of the building as erected (if built subsequent to the adoption of local by-laws). On the other hand, many local authorities destroyed early deposited plans on the reorganizations of local government in 1974 and 1986.
4. *Estate office archives.* Especially for buildings dating from the eighteenth century onwards, owners and estate offices often have comprehensive archives, including survey and architectural drawings, even where there has not been continuity of ownership.

The more important the building appears to be, the more likely it is that it will have generated records in the past. It must be recognized, however, that very many of the old buildings which will be encountered in day-to-day work possess no surviving documentation. Documentary research may often be best contracted out to a specialist, whose knowledge of likely sources and of how to use them can save a great deal of time. In approaching a specialist documentary researcher, it is essential to brief him or her as fully as possible about the nature of the enquiry and the kind of information that is likely to be useful.

ANALYSIS OF THE HISTORIC STRUCTURE

It has been said already that the essence of the record lies in coming to an understanding of the building and of its development and structure, and that all recording should have as its objective the elucidation and illustration of this understanding. This process has been called 'analytical recording' – it involves a close examination of the building, during which the building recorder seeks to disentangle its history using the many strands of evidence and the many analytical techniques available to him. The building recorder knows the kind of questions he wishes to answer – about how the building was built, how it developed and how it was used – and he knows, too, the sort of evidence that is most likely to contribute to this understanding. The following are some of the most useful of the approaches that the analytical recorder employs; some of these points are expanded in Appendix I:

- Archaeological method: primarily, the identification of structural sequences by recognizing the logic of construction – by understanding that one part of a building must necessarily pre- or post-date another. This is the fundamental technique whereby one identifies the relative (as opposed to the absolute) dating of different parts of a structure.
- Assessment of the most likely explanation for structural features: for straight joints, blocked openings, changes in masonry types, empty mortices, etc. A great many such features (and there are several more of similar kind) are susceptible of more than one explanation, and it is important to remain open-minded to all possible interpretations. No one explanation will be right in all cases (Figure 33).
- Recognition of the economy of a structure: the distinction between necessary and redundant structure and mass. Redundant work (e.g. inexplicably thick walls or a roof truss apparently out of sequence) may be secondary or may be a partial survival from an earlier phase of building.
- Recognition of the characteristics of the materials employed, and of what they are and are not likely to have been used for.
- Recognition that a feature of a building that may now be inexplicable could be explained by presupposing another structure, now demolished, of which no traces have otherwise been noted (and for which confirmatory evidence should now be sought).
- Recognition of evidence for related structures now destroyed (irrespective of the above).
- Recognizing when materials have been re-used, and when possible identifying their source (particularly if these are from elsewhere in the same building or in a predecessor).
- Distinguishing between primary and secondary decoration.
- Recognition of the functional logic of a building: that it was built to work in a certain way for the convenience of those who used it, and that in its successive stages of development it will have been altered to meet changing functional needs.
- Recognition of a hierarchy of spaces in a building, which may be identified directly by degrees of decoration or by external ornament, and indirectly by the position of rooms on the plan and their position in the circulatory system.
- Identification of the functional spaces normally to be met with in a building of well-recognized type (e.g. Hall, Great Chamber, etc.).
- Recognition of evidence for absolute dating.
- Identification of elements which may be explained through the employment of specialized techniques; for example, by remote sensing in order to gain access to concealed areas, by dendrochronology in order to reach an absolute date for the building, by reference of stone and mortar samples to experts for the identification of their sources, or by the employment of appropriate specialists (e.g. below-ground archaeologists).

Figure 33 Newton Hall, Yorkshire; photograph of the exterior showing blocked mullioned and transomed windows

And finally, the synthesis of all the material evidence suggested by the consideration of these points into a coherent account of the building's history. It sometimes happens that even the most expert building historian is beaten at the end of the day: some buildings are of such complexity, or the evidence for their history is so baffling, so inaccessible or else just so partial, that a coherent story is not possible. When that happens, one can do no more than record the evidence as it is, hoping that subsequent work (or even a more perceptive recorder!) can make sense of it at a later date.

(It may be worth adding a word of warning. In analysing the origin and development of the building, many architectural historians find a natural inclination to value its original form above subsequent developments and alterations. It is obviously very important to try to discover what the building was like originally – this must be one's starting point for the understanding of what happened later. But the later changes may be just as important and equally interesting.)

GRAPHIC AND OTHER VISUAL TECHNIQUES

While the understanding of the building is basic to the record, there are a number of graphic and visual techniques by which the analysis should be illustrated. The very exercise of these techniques often illuminates the building's history: the close examination of the structure that they may require may compel one to notice things that one had not noticed before, while the exact measurement of wall alignments, of angles and of wall thicknesses may raise questions and suggest solutions that one was not previously aware of. These graphic and visual techniques are briefly described below.

Dimensioned sketches and site notes

The dimensioned sketch is the simplest and quickest means of on-site recording. It consists simply of a freehand drawing – a plan, an elevation, a section or a perspective – on which the recorder has added certain basic dimensions that he wishes to record (Figure 34). Its advantages are speed, economy, the fact that any chosen viewpoint can be used, and consequently that by its use an impressionistic record can be made – which may have a number of useful applications – at very little cost. It is invaluable for the clear record of structural details, such as the joints of a timber-framed structure, where it is important to show accurately how a detail works without the necessity for recording every dimension. Moreover, it is particularly useful for recording industrial buildings and machinery, of which photographs alone are often confusing. Its major disadvantage, however, is that such a record can generate no more information than is recorded at the time, and calls for experience to do well. It is a technique to be used after one has reached one's understanding of a structure, not before.

Hand measurement

Hand measurement involves the direct measurement of a structure on site, and the preparation of scale drawings from the dimensions obtained. Hand measurement was until recently the only method available of producing an accurate, scale drawing of a building, and all the monuments of

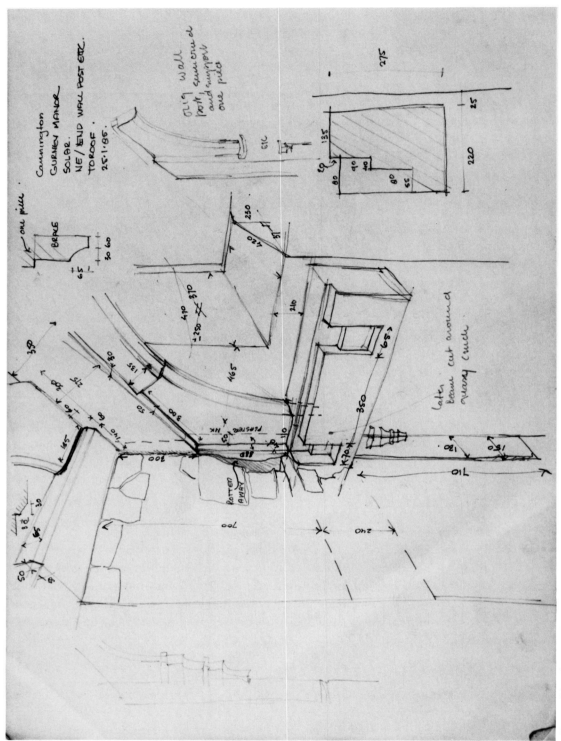

Figure 34 Gurney Street Manor, Cannington, Somerset; perspective sketch of the junction of roof and wall structure at the north end of the solar. This type of drawing, by an experienced recorder, conveys information on structure, condition and dimensions in a clear and succinct manner

antiquity whose records have formed the basis of the historical architectural styles of Europe were recorded in this way (Figure 35).

The great advantage of hand measurement is that it can be carried out, by those familiar with the techniques, without recourse to specialists or to specialized and expensive equipment. This means in addition that the practitioner – the architect, surveyor, planner, etc. – can himself control the extent and scope of the information he needs to record for any specific purpose, while the very process of measuring gives him a familiarity with the building that he can never achieve by studying records made by others. Nor are the techniques involved basically difficult.

Hand measurement is best suited to buildings of modest size, and difficulties may be met in measuring buildings that are badly deformed – with walls out of plumb or out of alignment, or with beams and roof timbers severely sagging. The need generally to gain physical access to points from which measurements are to be taken also poses difficulties in tackling large or tall buildings. Traditionally, equipment has comprised rods, tapes, chains, plumb lines, etc., but although instruments such as optic levels and range finders are now available, the use of which can greatly assist accuracy, the more sophisticated of these are not cheap. Nevertheless, the accuracy that can be achieved over long distances by the use of such items makes hand measurement, supplemented by modern electronic surveying equipment and the use of computer-aided design (CAD), the simplest and most accurate means of generating plans of large and complex structures (Figures 36–38).

Hand measurement is expensive in time and manpower. At least two people, preferably three, are needed if the work is to be done with the greatest efficiency. There is a danger in the hands of inexperienced operators of leaving out key measurements without which the rest of the record cannot be drawn up. It is not well suited to the storage of raw data, although this is frequently done in the form of field notes to be referred to later at need: the reason for this is that the accuracy of the dimensions recorded can only be confirmed when the record is drawn up in the office and all measurements taken are integrated and reconciled. Hand measurement is often invaluable for filling in essential data unrecorded by other techniques (such as by photography) or where by their employment small-scale detail could only be recorded at disproportionate cost (e.g. by photogrammetry).

Photography

Conventional photography is quick, versatile and generally easy to carry out. Only one person is usually needed on site, and close access to the object to be recorded is generally not essential. It also, more than any other technique, preserves the impression received by the human eye. It is ideal when a very comprehensive visual record is needed, for a progress record during the course of work, when time is very limited, or where access is difficult or disruption of work in progress has to be kept to a minimum. It is also invaluable to show the actual appearance of a building and the relationship of its elements (Figures 39 and 40), to show the effect of a decorative scheme, or to show the initial appearance to a detail that is to be restored.

There are, however, drawbacks. The camera is not wholly objective: distortions do occur, notably when using wide-angle lenses and when tilting the camera, that falsify the proportions of what is being photographed (for this reason, drawings should never be made directly from photographs). Accurate measurement is impossible, even though a scale should be incorporated into pictures wherever appropriate. Small-scale detail whose significance may be clear on site, seen

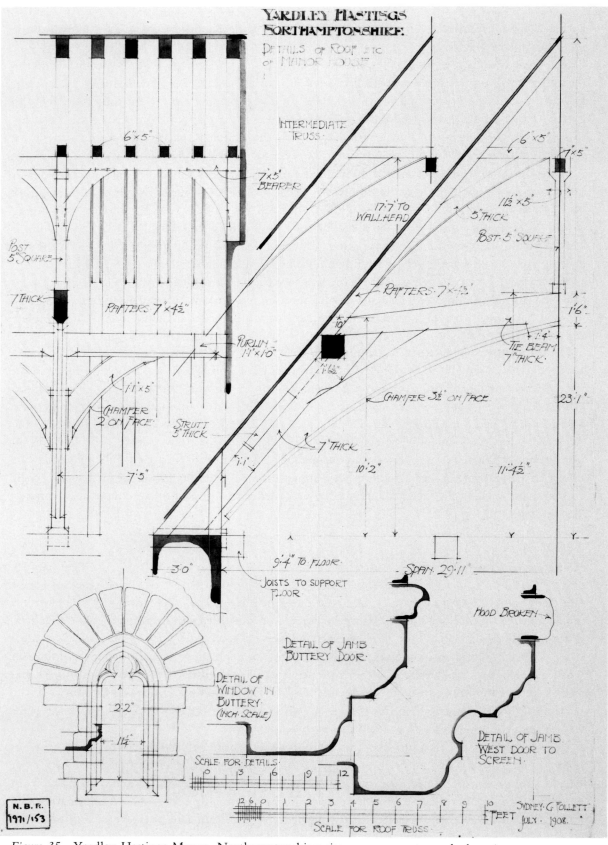

Figure 35 Yardley Hastings Manor, Northamptonshire; site measurements worked up into an accurate, fully dimensioned and at the same time visually pleasing structural drawing (1908)

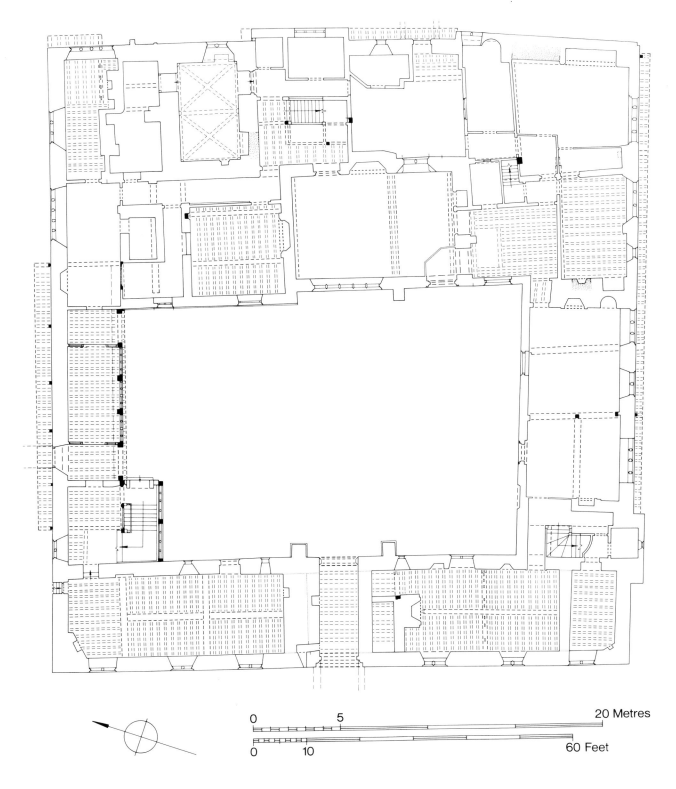

0 5   20 Metres

0 10   60 Feet

IGHTHAM MOTE

PLAN OF THE GROUND FLOOR

Figure 36 Ightham Mote, Kent; ground floor plan prepared by EDM (Electronic Distance Measurement) combined with hand survey. The use of electronic equipment overcomes the problems which might jeopardize the accuracy of a survey of so irregular a plan by hand measurement alone

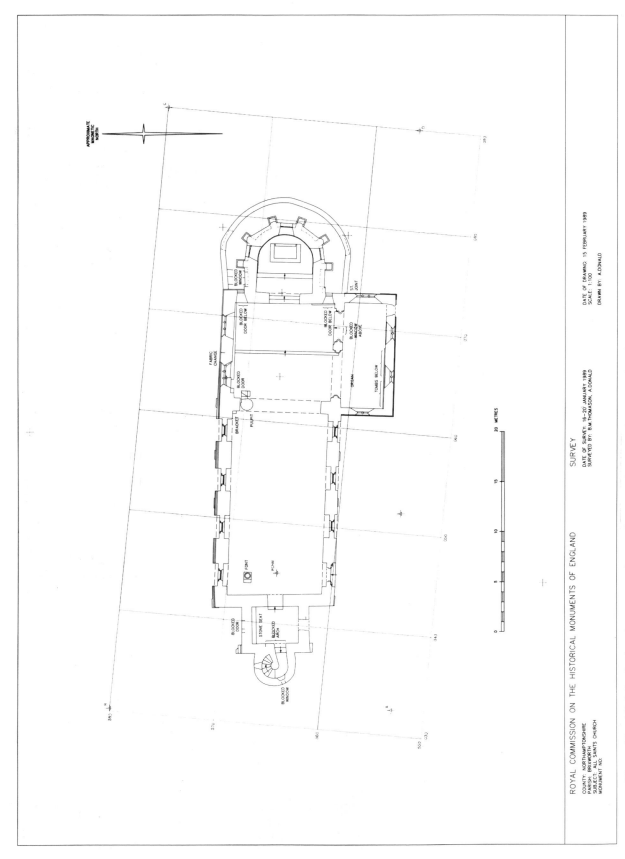

ROYAL COMMISSION ON THE HISTORICAL MONUMENTS OF ENGLAND

COUNTY: NORTHAMPTONSHIRE
PARISH: BRIXWORTH
SUBJECT: ALL SAINTS CHURCH
MONUMENT NO:

SURVEY

DATE OF SURVEY: 16-20 JANUARY 1989
SURVEYED BY: B.M.THOMASON, A.DONALD

DATE OF DRAWING: 15 FEBRUARY 1989
SCALE: 1:100

DRAWN BY: A.DONALD

Figure 37 All Saints' Church, Brixworth, Northamptonshire; another example of a plan survey carried out using EDM equipment

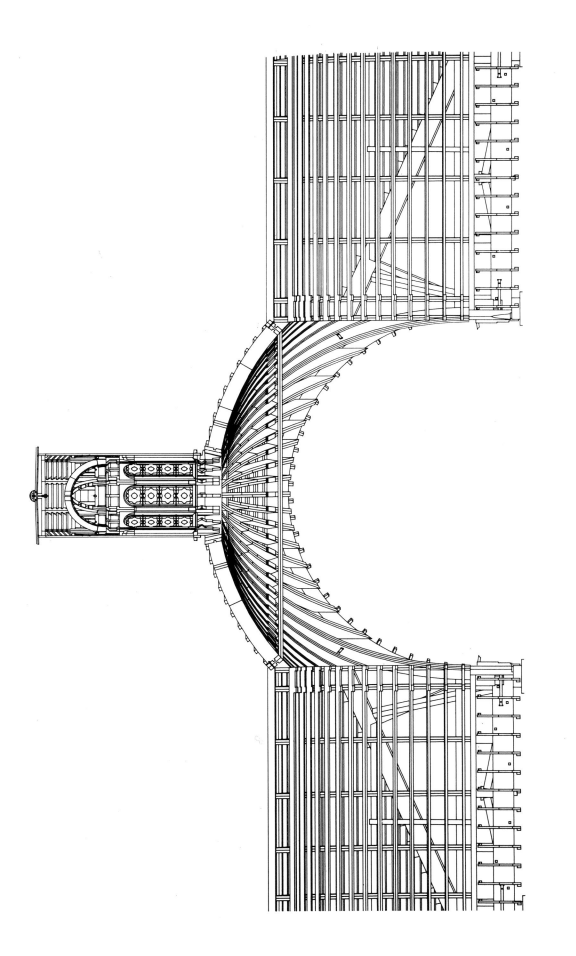

Figure 38 Church of St. Mary-at-Hill, City of London; section through the roof, dome and lantern. A section plotted using CAD technology, which is particularly suited to the projection of complex structures employing compound curves

0   5 m

Figure 39 Barn at Walton, Peterborough, Cambridgeshire; photograph of surviving members of the structural frame. To record such a deformed structure by drawing would be practically impossible; the camera records the essential features of the structure and its jointing and assembly

Figure 40 59 High Street, Buntingford, Hertfordshire; photograph of the corner of a room. The photograph readily conveys the nature, materials and form of a rediscovered early doorway formed in the timber frame and subsequently blocked

in context, may be inexplicable when photographed alone, and the apparent objectivity of the image does not remove the need for careful annotation of pictures. While colour photography has obvious uses, black-and-white must be preferred for archival permanence whenever appropriate processing can be achieved (although this is often not available from standard commercial processors). Filters can sometimes be used to highlight detail, such as decorative or material changes, that would otherwise be undifferentiated in monochrome.

Lighting can be a problem, particularly indoors. Camera-mounted flash guns tend to flatten the image and to lose relief; the length of exposures often needed in low-light situations means that a tripod is essential for mounting the camera, and long exposures encounter the technical problem known as 'reciprocity failure', when indicated exposure times cease to be reliable. The small format, 35 mm camera generally available to amateurs can seldom produce a print larger than 10 in × 8 in (or proportionate enlargements from smaller areas of negative) without an unacceptable 'graininess' or coarsening of detail.

Recourse to professional photographers should always be had when the circumstances warrant it: the professional has equipment and expertise that can cope with most situations and can make possible a greatly improved record. On the other hand, he must be told carefully what to record – few professional photographers, even those who specialize in architectural photography, are expert in the comprehension of buildings in the sense in which it is being discussed in these pages.

Rectified photography

Rectified photography involves making a true-to-scale photographic print of an object such as the facade of a building (Figures 41 and 42). Dimensions can then be scaled off this photograph with reasonable accuracy. Single photographs may be made, or a mosaic of several photographs can be composed. Photographic prints are normally made onto transparent film so that dyeline copies may be taken. The process is simple, but it has certain limitations.

The advantages of rectified photography are that it is quick and easy to prepare, it produces a detailed photographic image from which a great deal of information may be derived, and it can be practised with ordinary photographic equipment of good quality by anyone reasonably competent with a camera.

The main disadvantages are limitations on accuracy, which are very difficult to check unless by recourse to an alternative means of recording, e.g. by hand measurement. There may also be difficulties in reproducing the half-tone image by normal dyeline processes. On site, the elevation of the building must be flat. If it has substantial projections or recesses, this will lead to scale and displacent effects in the photography and to possibly serious inaccuracies. Window reveals of, say, 150 mm depth will present no serious problems, but a projecting buttress a metre deep will be seriously out of scale and position. Further, the camera must be lined up very carefully so that it is exactly parallel to the facade in both horizontal and vertical planes, while there must be no significant distortion in the camera or in the enlarger lenses.

54

Figure 41   Mortimer's Cross Water Mill, Herefordshire; an elevation recorded by rectified photography. This technique is especially suited to simple rectilinear buildings with few changes of elevational plane. Figure 42 shows that, where a reasonable camera location cannot be found, part of the elevation has to be indicated in another manner

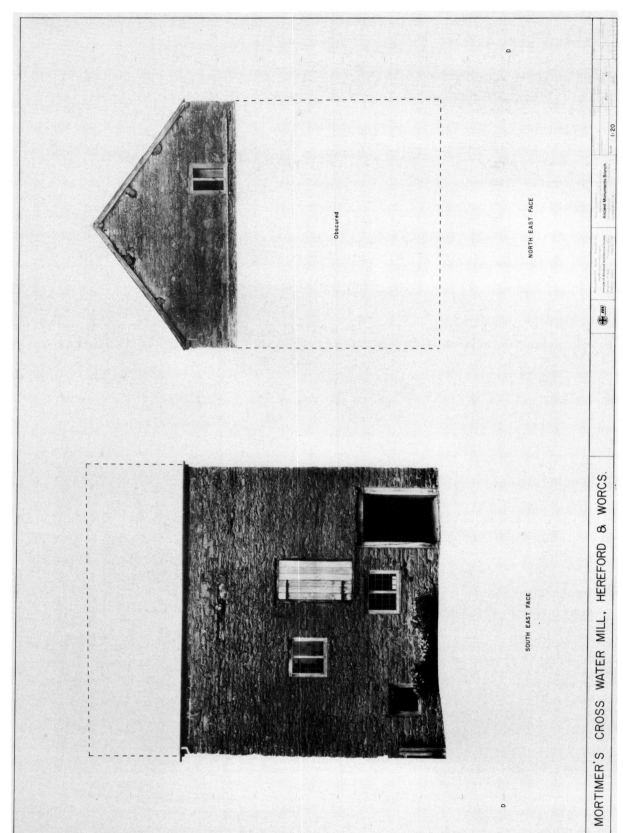

MORTIMER'S CROSS WATER MILL, HEREFORD & WORCS.

SOUTH EAST FACE

NORTH EAST FACE

Obscured

Figure 42   See Figure 41

Photogrammetry

Photogrammetry is a means of producing drawings by measurement from photography. Most commonly used in the preparation of line drawings of facades, it can have other applications. Essentially, a three-dimensional image is produced by stereoscopic photography from which accurate measurement can be made (Figure 43). It is a two-step operation, involving on-site photography with a 'metric' camera, with accurately calibrated lenses of known property, and then a plotting process using photogrammetric plotting equipment in the surveyor's office.

The great advantage of photogrammetry over rectified photography is that full allowance can be made for variations in the recession of a facade – in the distance of its parts from the recorder. The method is ideally suited to making accurate drawings of large and/or complex structures such as traceried windows, irregular masonry, etc., and the level of detail recorded is entirely at the discretion of the recorder (Figure 44). Three-dimensional information is available, so that cross-sections or the contour of a bulging wall can easily be measured.

Photogrammetry presents good value for money if its full potential is exploited – if it is employed for purposes where other techniques would be inadequate or prohibitively time consuming, but it would be generally too expensive to use on small or simple facades, or when only a low level of accuracy or only a few key measurements were needed. The process depends, too, on the skill and knowledge not only of the recorder on site, but also of the plotter in the office, who must be made aware of the needs of the record user.

A further great advantage of photogrammetry is that it creates an archive of information that can be referred to later at need, in that the photographs themselves are a valuable source of information, whereas the second stage – the preparation of the drawing – need not be embarked on at once but at any time in the future. The process is also accurate, fast and safe, in so far as no physical contact is required with the structure (in this it resembles photography and rectified photography).

Disadvantages, besides the expense and the need for specialized equipment and trained operators, are that it is difficult to use in confined spaces or where significant detail is obscured, e.g. by scaffolding (it can record only what the camera sees). Although it can be used to generate plans, it is not economically used for this purpose if this is the only end in view (Figure 45).

Other techniques

Other methods of recording may be used on occasion. A very full understanding of a building may be conveyed by a carefully planned tour with a video camera, accompanied by a written or spoken narrative account. On occasions, it may be easier on site to speak into a hand-held tape recorder than to make notes in a book. In such cases as these, the recordings made may usefully form a part of the record of the building to be preserved for reference later.

RECORDING NEW WORK

The previous paragraphs have been concerned with how to record the building that exists and in advance of work that is going to be done. It is, however, just as important to record the work that

Figure 43 Little Moreton Hall, Cheshire; stereo-photographs for photogrammetric survey. The stereoscopic effect of taking paired photographs from slightly different viewpoints forms the basis of the survey

Figure 44   Lichfield Cathedral, Staffordshire; a fully developed photogrammetric survey of the west end

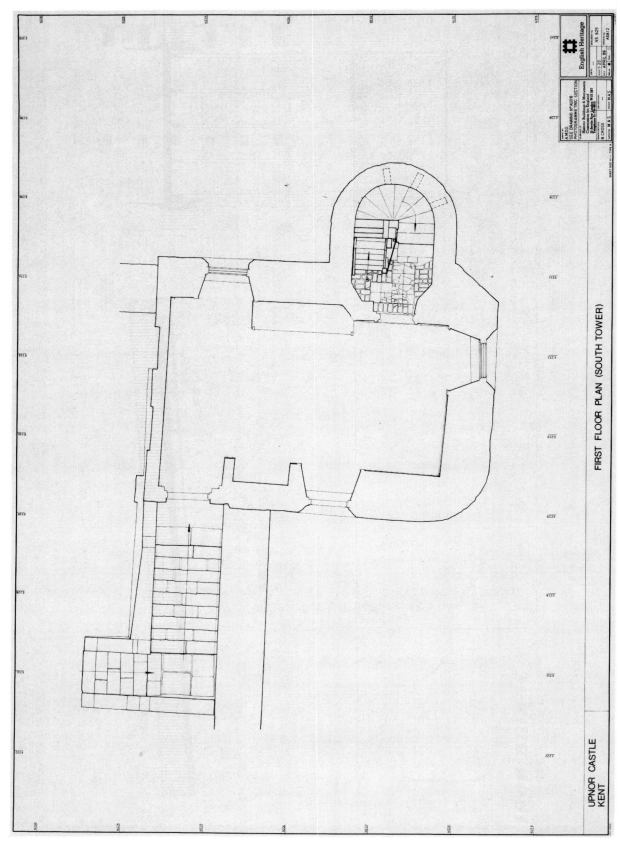

UPNOR CASTLE
KENT

FIRST FLOOR PLAN (SOUTH TOWER)

Figure 45 Upnor Castle, Kent; photogrammetric plan, demonstrating that this method of survey can be used to generate plans as well as elevations, provided that appropriate camera locations are accessible

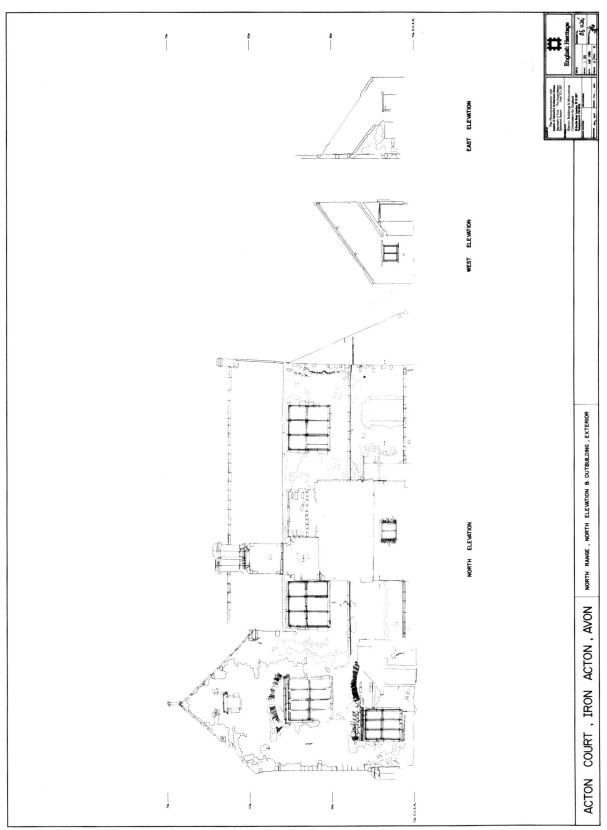

NORTH ELEVATION

WEST ELEVATION

EAST ELEVATION

ACTON COURT , IRON ACTON , AVON

NORTH RANGE , NORTH ELEVATION & OUTBUILDING , EXTERIOR

English Heritage

Figure 46 Acton Court, Iron Acton, Avon; records taken during a programme of consolidation works. This figure shows the north range, north elevation photogrammetric survey base. Figure 47 shows the same survey drawing augmented with hand-drawn information and annotated to identify materials, etc. Figure 48 shows a similarly augmented survey of part of the interior. See also Figures 49 and 50

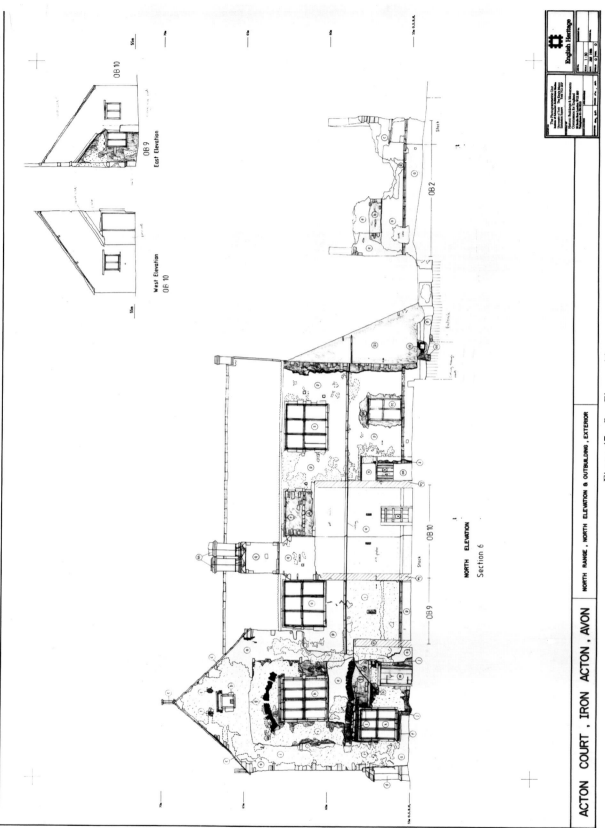

ACTON COURT , IRON ACTON , AVON | NORTH RANGE , NORTH ELEVATION & OUTBUILDING , EXTERIOR

Figure 47 See Figure 46

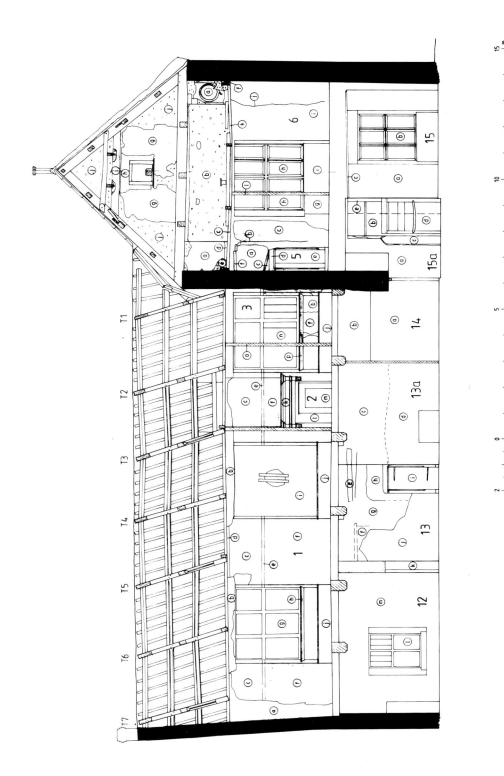

ACTON COURT
Section 11

Figure 48 See Figure 46

East

West

R 87

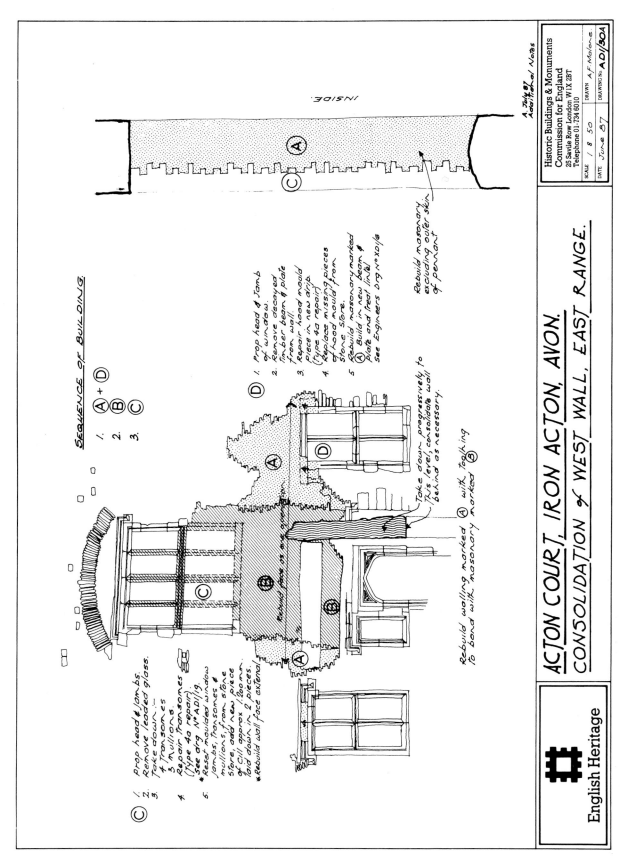

Figure 49 Acton Court, Iron Acton, Avon; detail of part of the east range, west wall. An enlargement of part of the survey elevation amended and annotated to give instructions for work to be carried out, including the sequence of work. A further example (Figure 50) shows the remedial work needed to a buttress on the east elevation of the same range. See also Figures 46–48

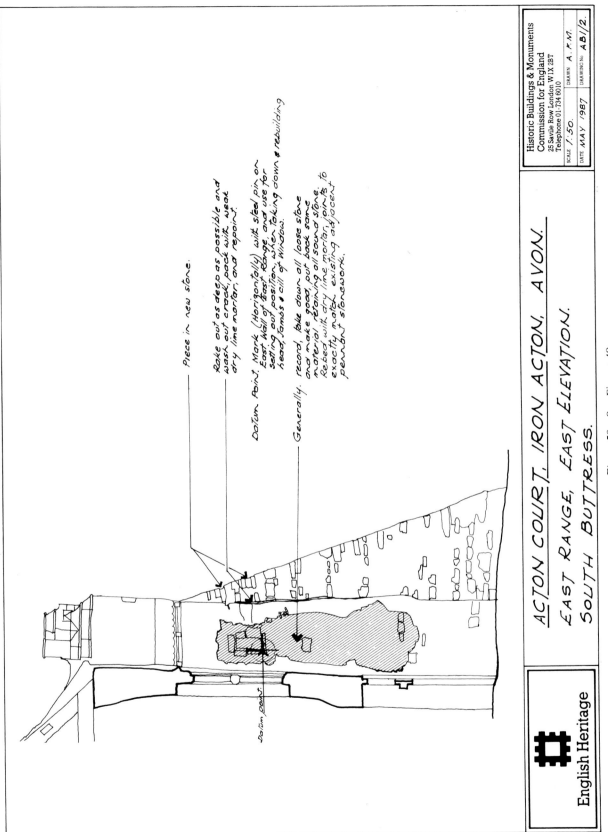

Figure 50   See Figure 49

is actually carried out (Figures 46–50). The most convenient way of doing this will be by means of the documents that the work itself generates: by means of drawings, specifications, technical reports and photographs of work in progress. This should be accompanied by a sufficiently detailed narrative, describing what work was done, why it was needed, who it was done for, any particular technical difficulties encountered or novel techniques that were employed, and any other facts that a successor owner, architect, contractor or conservationist might need in order to make sense of the contract documents that provide the essential facts. It is of the utmost importance, however, to note any departure from these contract documents. In practice, in more cases than not, discoveries and circumstances arising during the course of the work occasion a departure from the original plans and specification, and it is very easy to lose sight of these changes and to have forgotten them when, at the conclusion of the work, the time comes for putting together a record of it.

The most difficult cases are those where work is carried out without benefit of detailed specifications and drawings. Though for the most part these will be small jobs of routine maintenance and repair, often expedients will be resorted to and preservative techniques employed by a contractor called in for the purpose, of which virtually no record would normally be made. Nor, in such cases, is the client commissioning the work likely to have the benefit of advice on an appropriate record. All that can be urged is that surveyors and architects ought to try to impress on their client that, when in the future he commissions work from a contractor without recourse to professional advice, he should find out as accurately as he can what his contractor has done, and keep safely whatever notes and records he can make on the occasion.

CHAPTER 5

WHO?

CARRYING OUT THE INITIAL SURVEY

The person making the preliminary record of the building will often not be the one who is responsible for making (or correlating) the record of the work done. The ideal person to make the initial record is the person who will have to take the decisions about what is to be done to it – what alterations may be compatible with its historic character, how necessary repairs can be carried out while at the same time respecting the integrity of its structure, and what new decoration may be possible while not destroying anything of historic interest. Such a person would ideally be the building's owner (or at least the person responsible for it and for making decisions about its future) or else the architect who is to prepare specifications for the work to be done. In practice, however, owners seldom have the skills or knowledge for such work, while architects, even when they do possess such knowledge (and specialist training in the analysis of old buildings is not in fact generally available to architects) often lack the time: it is difficult to persuade clients that time spent on what may seem an elaborate initial survey is time spent productively. It will therefore often be the case, for all these reasons, that an outside body should be called on to undertake the record of a building before work starts.

The principal national body charged with the recording of historic buildings is the Royal Commission on Historical Monuments. Each of the three national Commissions (see Appendix II for their addresses) has the duty under successive Town and Country Planning Acts to record listed historic buildings before they are to be demolished, in whole or in part, but on occasions they may wish, or may be invited, to make a record of a building before decisions have been reached on what may become of it. The reports made by the Royal Commissions' expert architectural staff can be of the greatest value if the building is to be altered or restored. On the other hand, the Royal Commissions have limited staff resources, and many other tasks to perform, and there will be many occasions when it is necessary to employ other recorders.

There is a number of local Archaeological Excavation Units operating throughout the British Isles. Some of these units (though not all of them) have been recording buildings for many years and may be asked for advice or for active help. A unit would normally expect to charge for its services.

Throughout the country, there are architectural historians active in the analytical recording of historic buildings. Their competence varies, and though much may be learnt through personal recommendation, the safest way of assessing their skills is by taking a copy of an existing record and testing it against a standing building. There is a growing number of people who are recording buildings or carrying out historical research upon them, professionally, although there is as yet no central body through whom these professional recorders can be approached. Some of them advertise in relevant periodicals. The English Royal Commission on Historical Monuments has published its *Survey of Architectural Surveys*, which is a list of those historic building recorders that are known to it. Many active recorders belong to the Vernacular Architecture Group (for address see Appendix II), although most of its members record buildings for their own interest, and may be unwilling to accept specific commissions, while their expertise generally lies with the humbler buildings – the vernacular buildings of a particular area. None the less they represent a great body of knowledge which should be drawn upon whenever appropriate.

A number of County and District Councils employ conservation officers to exercise controls over the historic building stock and to advise planning committees on the exercise of their powers. It is seldom that such officers are themselves able to make full records of a building, but their inspection of it may often have led them to recognize important historic elements that should be regarded in any scheme, while their local knowledge may enable them to recommend some person or organization with the resources to undertake a proper record. It is in any case always advisable to have a preliminary, informal discussion with the appropriate conservation officer before undertaking any work for which the Council's Listed Building Consent will be required.

Most dioceses and most cathedrals have archaeological consultants, who should be the first people to turn to for advice, and sometimes for practical help, in arranging archaeological recording of the churches of the Church of England. Information and advice is also to be had from Diocesan Advisory Committees – the standing committees in each diocese whose duty is to advise the church authorities on the historical and artistic implications of the grant of faculties (which are necessary for all structural work to the fabric of a church in use).

Some building recorders deposit their records in local Record Offices, which may also be a source of information about such people. Increasingly, too, the need for records and the curiosity of house owners is creating a demand for professional building historians, some of whom advertise in periodicals dealing with old buildings. Once again, however, the expertise of such people must not be taken on trust; some may be tempted to make an old building appear more interesting and important than it really is and to find in it historic features it may not actually possess.

RECORDING THE WORK UNDERTAKEN

Recording the work done in execution of a contract ought to be the duty of whoever is supervising the contract, and in most cases of the kind that this book is considering this will be the architect. In addition to ensuring that whatever work he has been directly responsible for is recorded with whatever drawings, specifications and descriptive account seem appropriate to any likely demands in the future, he should make sure that whatever sub-contract he may have authorized, whatever work was placed with specialists – with structural engineers, conservationists, preservative treatment firms, and so forth – is fully recorded. The level of record can best be determined by the question, 'Who in the future is likely to want to know what?', and the same question must determine the points to be made in the next part of this book. It may seem obvious, but it is perhaps worth making the point that it is futile to make a record that cannot be preserved.

CHAPTER 6

WHERE?

PRESERVING THE RECORD

To make the fullest and finest record possible is obviously pointless, except for the recorder, if nobody else thereafter is going to be able to use it. The question of who is to use and who is to maintain and preserve the record is one that should be faced at the very outset, rather than left until the work is done, the record made, and no one can be found to look after it.

The records to be preserved are, of course, of two kinds – those made as part of the initial appraisal and survey, and those generated as a result of the work carried out. The first record will often be manageable: it will comprise a written account of the building, backed up by drawings and photographs that will not usually amount to a very bulky dossier. In the latter case, however – the documents that record what was actually done – some selection will almost certainly be needed: it is unreasonable to expect anyone to keep all the papers generated in the course of a job, and the object should be to reduce the archive (which is what the accumulation of papers will form) to a level that combines the preservation of essential information with what it is practical to preserve.

In the case of those records of a building that are the result of the initial survey, wherever possible consideration should be given to depositing them for safe keeping in a public archive. This will ensure not only their efficient management, but also that they are available to anyone in the future who may have a legitimate concern with the building and who requires further information about it. Nationally, the body to be considered is the National Buildings Record (see Chapter 4); locally, the appropriate County Record Office. In addition, most local authorities maintain a Sites and Monuments Record (SMR), comprising information about the historic and environmental resources of the area for use as a planning tool. The level of information required by different SMRs differs from one to another, but planning or conservation officers should always be approached and asked whether they will accept records for deposit in the local SMR.

A copy of the initial record should always be lodged with the owner or occupier of the building, so that it is on hand for reference at any time. This is particularly so in the case of those buildings – e.g. institutional buildings of any kind – where repairs and minor works are liable to be carried out by non-expert staff, and where the building manager should be able to refer to an expert appraisal of the structure to see whether what is proposed will have a damaging effect on it.

For the records of work done in the course of a contract, the national repository of contemporary architectural drawings and related documents of all kinds is the British Architectural Library of the RIBA. The policy of the library is to collect material of national or international importance; it may not therefore be able to find space for all records that are offered to it.

Some local record offices have a more active policy than others in collecting the drawings and working papers of local architectural firms or those relating to buildings in their area. The RIBA and the English Royal Commission on Historical Monuments have jointly produced a booklet, *Architectural Records in National and Local Collections – Guidance Notes for Archivists and Record Offices* (free from the librarian of either organization) which offers advice to those responsible for local collections and which lists those documents that are most likely to be of permanent value.

In the case of the public archives already described, help or guidance will be offered on what it is desirable to preserve (within the archives' own terms of reference). In some cases the work will have been undertaken for institutions such as the church or the National Trust, whose permanence and size make it possible for them to preserve the archive and whose management system should ensure that it is not lost sight of. In other cases, where the record is to be preserved privately, it will need to be ordered and a selection made of essential material so that it can readily be used in the future. Indeed, if the architect does not do this himself, the archive is unlikely to be used, since the difficulty of finding in it the information that may be needed will probably deter anyone from trying. An architect will recognize that the endurance of the work he was responsible for depends on its being looked after, and that to prepare an archive of this kind ought therefore to be a part of his job. It has to be realized that this responsibility may impose a good deal of additional work on the architect (or whoever prepared the specifications and supervised the work). For some complex jobs, even a reduced archive will still amount to a great deal of paper.

The alternatives to public repositories for the deposit and preservation of records are (a) the body or individual commissioning the work, (b) the architect, and (c) the recorder, where an outside recorder has been involved.

The building's owner

This ought to be the best solution, since the records should thus be available at the building when they are required, and the building's owner should have an interest in keeping them safely. An owner who is interested in the history of his house is quite likely to want to keep an initial survey, if it includes (as it should) an account of the probable origins and subsequent development of the building. The problem becomes greater in relation to the mass of documents that are often created in the course of a contract for alterations, extensions or for major repairs.

Even if owners are conscientious in keeping them (which cannot be guaranteed), it is impossible to be sure that records will be passed on to successive owners and preserved. Many private owners these days have in their own possession no legal document relating to their house, and it is unrealistic for a sheaf of drawings and specifications to be lodged with deeds held by a building society. The answers may be (a) for an owner to be encouraged to keep a building logbook, in which all significant work is noted down, which can be passed on to his successor and which by its existence can remind him of other papers to be passed on as well; and (b) where it is practicable, for a summary of what has been done (a summary account was suggested in Chapter 4) to be attached to the deeds, together with a record of the architect or contractor involved. Similar documents, such as the guarantees issued by preservative treatment firms, are often attached in such a way. But it has to be recognized that none of this is ideal, and that a great many owners will fail to see the value of preserving papers that relate to building work long after the likelihood of further repair or remedial works has passed.

The architect

An architect will generally keep records of a contract for as long as may be necessary for insurance purposes, and frequently long after that. If the procedures recommended here are followed, the architect will have in his possession records made before the commencement of the work, and records made in the course of it. If someone other than the architect (a specialist building recorder or someone acting for the contractor) has been monitoring discoveries made during the contract, then just as it will have been for the architect to ensure that the record is made in the first place, so it should also be his responsibility to see that the record is preserved together with any other relevant contract papers. The same holds true for records made by conservators in the course of any specialist treatment.

Before finally disposing of records, the architect should try to contact the building's present owners and a national or local record office (see above) and suggest that they take over the documents that he no longer needs. If this is done, however, it should be made clear that the recipient understands the copyright position in the documents.

The building recorder

If the initial survey has been made by someone other than the architect, then this person will probably keep a copy (or the original) of his record. When he wishes finally to dispose of it, he should do so along the lines suggested in the preceding paragraph.

INTERPRETATIVE ELEMENTS

Analytical recording (described in Chapter 4) consists largely in the interpretation and subsequent record of the significant evidence for a building's original form and subsequent history that is contained within its fabric. This evidence consists of a wide variety of structural and decorative features, and the list below indicates some of those most frequently found useful in forming this analysis. Very much of this structural evidence relates to change; on the other hand, it is largely through the recognition of change (or its absence) that the original form of the building can be arrived at.

(At the same time, one must avoid the temptation to believe that the original form of a building is either the most interesting or the one to which it should be restored. Most buildings show a continuous evolution which is itself of interest. Without an elucidation of its history, one cannot properly appraise the effect of any proposals, but this elucidation does not, of itself, solve any of the problems that are properly those of the architect and client today. All work on old buildings is a balance of the claims of efficiency and authenticity.)

Evidence of multiple periods or phases of building

1. *Differences in material* (but may indicate only a repair, or the employment of a material better suited to a particular location in the building).
   2. *Breaks in masonry* (ditto). Notice should be taken of the precise form of the break (ragged or straight; whether aligned with internal partitions, etc; whether a true fabric change or a blocked opening (see below). It is not always easy to recognize at a junction which is the earlier of the two fabrics.
   3. *Adjoining parts of a building structurally independent of each other.* It may not always be possible to deduce which was built first.
   4. *Differences in wall alignment* (even if superficially the fabric appears similar).
   5. *Differences in wall thickness* (ditto). Such differences may relate to differences in function – e.g. the need for a load-bearing structure or the incorporation of a vanished flue – rather than to differences of period.
   6. *Differences in structural techniques.* There are changes over time in brickwork, timber framing, roof construction, etc.
   7. *Stylistic differences in architecture and decoration* (although decoration may itself be secondary; evidence for structural alteration should be looked for as well).

8. *Evidence for the demolition of part of a building* (without its replacement by a later structure). This will often be shown in a masonry building by irregularities at angles or of coursing. In a timber building it may be shown by inadequate support to horizontal members, by empty mortices, or by untypical structural treatment at angles. In all cases it may be suggested by anomalies in plan, by blocked openings that cannot otherwise be explained, or by the use of a different material in making good the area demolished.

9. *Documentary sources* (although evidence to support the implications of documentary evidence should always be sought in the structure itself).

Blocked openings – doors and windows

These are vital indications of the building's former appearance and method of use:

1. *Alterations indicated in masonry buildings* – by changes in material, by breaks in coursing of stone or brick, by vertical lines of closers in brickwork, by breaks in plinths in stone or brick, by former door or window heads remaining *in situ* (although in stone buildings beware of interpreting relieving arches as former door or window heads, even though they may relate to such openings).

2. *Alterations indicated in timber-framed buildings* – by empty mortices for door heads and window sills in posts and studs; by empty sockets in wall plates and in cross-rails for window mullions, and grooves for sliding window shutters; by breaks in lines of studs or of stud mortices at the site of a former door opening; by wear in sill beams at former thresholds; by inserted studs, to block openings, that are not properly morticed into the members at foot and head.

Inserted openings in masonry buildings

These may be shown by a lack of finish at the jambs (an absence of quoins or closers, or by a break in the coursing where quoins or closers have been inserted). In timber-framed buildings, these openings may be shown by posts and studs cut into the members at head or foot, without true tenons or pegs (if present elsewhere in the building), or by unsupported ends of cross-rails where these abut the insertion. Inserted doors and windows (like other decoration) are likely to be in a style corresponding to the date of their insertion rather than in that of the original fabric, although not infrequently earlier door and window surrounds may be moved to other positions.

Plan alterations

Internal alterations may be shown by the following:

1. *Evidence for alteration of partition walls.* This can be shown by changes in the form of, or the partial absence of, cornices (although cornices may be reproduced, and their absence may simply indicate partial damage); by other interrupted schemes of decoration (e.g. ceiling decoration that seems not to fit the room it serves); by scars in the fabric of structural walls where partitions abutted them; by empty mortices for wall studs in the soffit of cross-beams. Openings of later date than the original structure may indicate that the partitions containing them are also of that date.

2. *Evidence from present or former openings.* The arrangement of openings may not clearly relate to the present internal divisions; alternatively, the present plan may only work in relation to openings that have been altered from their original form or position.

3. *Evidence of flues and fireplaces.* A room may be served by more than one flue; if so, it is possible that it has been formed by throwing two rooms together. If one such flue has been inserted, then the room may have been subdivided and later restored to its original form. (It is not safe to date a flue by the style of its chimney-piece, unless there is other structural or stylistic evidence to confirm. Chimney-pieces are among the decorative features most altered and introduced.) The number of flues is itself no safe evidence for the removal of a fireplace; fireplaces were sometimes built with multiple flues, and chimney stacks are occasionally dummies, built for show.

4. *Evidence for staircases.* This is most often to be found as a trimmer joist framing the opening formerly occupied by a stair. Removed staircases sometimes leave structural scars against walls. Cellar stairs, if present, are often the least altered, and can suggest the position of former staircases on floors above. The windows to stairs often cut floor levels; a blocked window in such a position is generally an indication of a former stair, although stairs were sometimes built across windows at normal height.

5. *Evidence for inserted passages.* This will usually be a combination of the evidence for alterations to partitions, together with the evidence for altered doors. Their insertion will often have made necessary changes to windows, on account of the need to light both the passage and the room out of which it was formed.

6. *Decoration.* Decoration itself does not provide a guide to alteration, although (if genuinely of the period which it purports to be) it provides a *terminus ad quem* for the structure to which it is applied. If a secondary (non-original) scheme of decoration is very extensive, then it may indicate other substantial work undertaken at the same period. Decoration, however, is always a principal indication of the use of a structure and of the status of the rooms within it, at the period at which the scheme was introduced.

7. *Conservatism.* Through the successive alterations in the long history of an old building, it is helpful to realize that certain things change less than others. Thus in a house, the position of kitchens and services often remains the same from the original form, though extensively altered in detail. The position of principal stairs is often unchanged, even though stairs, as major decorative as well as functional elements, are frequently essentially replaced. Alternate rebuilding of the parts of a house (e.g. in one generation the services, in another the family rooms) may preserve the relationship of its elements from a date to which virtually nothing of the existing fabric now relates.

Other evidence for structural form and alterations

1. *Inserted floors.* These are a frequent occurrence in medieval domestic buildings, and in some industrial structures as well. Evidence in a timber-framed building can often be that the ends of main beams carrying the inserted floor are imperfectly tenoned into the posts that carry them, and that the building shows other signs (which may be of many different sorts) of having originally been open from ground floor to roof. Floors can sometimes be renewed, and such new floors need to be carefully distinguished from inserted ones.

2. *Roofs.* If structurally sound, roofs often survive from an early period in the building's history;

there is no reason, either of function or of fashion, to replace them unless they are rotten, and they often provide an invaluable indication of the building's former status, its date, form and use. The forms of old roofs differ widely over time and place, and even if no work is being undertaken that will affect them, the forms of old roof trusses should always be recorded and any constructional details – the forms of joints, the presence of chamfers on members, etc. – carefully drawn.

Evidence for date

Evidence for the date of a building or its components will be in part relative, in part absolute. Absolute dating is when a firm date (or at least a close approximation) can be obtained from documents, from datable decoration in the building or from inscriptions. Such dating must always be regarded critically, however. Dates on buildings can be falsified, or may relate to a phase of ownership rather than of construction. The reproduction of period features can be misleadingly authentic, particularly if it took place long enough ago for the work to have acquired a patina or if it relates to a period with which the recorder is not totally familiar.

The meaning of dates and of wording in documents must be considered very carefully; certain phrases (such as 'that new building') may be repeated verbatim in legal formulas over very many years, while title deeds relate to property rather than to a specific building that was standing on a plot at any particular time. Builders or owners named in documents connected with a building are not necessarily the people who occupied it. Traditional errors can be repeated from one source to another, and human memory is notoriously fallible.

Relative dating is the relation of the building's parts to each other; much of the building recorder's work will depend on the establishment of such relative chronologies for the development of the building, and in the final analysis the dates assigned to a structure will depend on a combination of both absolute and relative dating.

SOME USEFUL ADDRESSES

The recording functions of the Royal Commissions on Historical Monuments and National Monuments Records are referred to on page 67. The archival functions of the National Monuments Records are described on page 69.

For England: *Royal Commission on the Historical Monuments of England/National Monuments Record*
Fortress House, 23 Savile Row, London W1X 1AB
Tel: 071-973 3000

For Scotland: *Royal Commission on the Ancient and Historical Monuments of Scotland/National Monuments Record*
54 Melville Street, Edinburgh EH3 7HF
Tel: 031-225 5994

For Wales: *Royal Commission on Ancient and Historical Monuments in Wales/National Monuments Record*
Crown Building, Plas Cruig, Aberystwyth, Dyfed SY23 2HP
Tel: 0970 624381

Contact with archaeologists in practice and with the regional archaeological units operating in various areas of the country can be obtained through:

The Council for British Archaeology
112 Kennington Road, London SE11 6RE
Tel: 071-582 0494

There is no organization to which building recorders, professional or otherwise, are generally affiliated, but many of those who record traditional buildings for their own interest belong to:

The Vernacular Architecture Group
18 Portland Place, Leamington Spa, Warwickshire CV32 5EU
Tel: 0926 28161

the Secretary of which may be able to put enquiries in touch with members in their area; see page 68.

Many specialists in early industrial buildings – which often require specialist knowledge of the processes for which they were put if they are to be properly understood – belong to:

The Association for Industrial Archaeology
The Wharfage, Ironbridge, Telford, Shropshire TF8 7AW
Tel: 095 245 3522

English Heritage, whose proper title and address is

The Historic Buildings and Monuments Commission
Fortress House, 23 Savile Row, London W1X 1AB
Tel: 071-973 3000

is responsible for compiling the official Lists of buildings of architectural and historic interest, which when approved by the Secretary of State for the Environment form the basis for the legal protection of historic buildings in England. Two principal committees of English Heritage are the *Historic Buildings Advisory Committee* and the *Historic Areas Advisory Committee*, the bodies through which the State makes available repair grants to the owners of historic buildings. The *Ancient Monuments Advisory Committee* fulfils a similar function with regard to scheduled monuments and archaeology.

In Wales and Scotland, the parallel authorities are:

CADW
Brunel House, 2 Fitzalan Road, Cardiff CF2 1UY
Tel: 0222 465511

The Scottish Development Department
Headquarters: St Andrew's House, Edinburgh EH1 3DD
Tel: 031-556 8400

London office: Dover House, Whitehall, London SW1A 2AU
Tel: 071-270 3000

The following are the principal national amenity societies concerned for the care and preservation of historic buildings. All of these, together with the Royal Commission on the Historical Monuments of England and the Council for British Archaeology (see above), have to be notified by Local Planning Authorities when an application is received by an LPA for Listed Building Consent to demolish a listed building in England, and may (save for the Royal Commission) wish to make observations on the application. In addition, the Secretaries of these societies may be able to provide the names and addresses of specialists on the buildings of the type and period with which each is concerned, who may be able to give advice.

The Ancient Monuments Society
St Andrews By The Wardrobe, Queen Victoria Street, London EC4V 5DE
Tel: 071-236 3934

The Society for the Protection of Ancient Buildings
37 Spital Square, London E1 6DY
Tel: 071-377 1644

The Georgian Group
37 Spital Square, London E1 6DY
Tel: 071-377 1644

The Victorian Society
1 Priory Gardens, Bedford Park, London W4 1TT
Tel: 081-994 1019

The concerns of the last two are implied in their names; the former are concerned with buildings of all periods, and the SPAB can often suggest architects specializing in historic buildings and specialist conservationists.

The following organizations are also concerned with those aspects of the recording of historic buildings implicit in their titles:

ICOMOS (The International Council on Monuments and Sites)
10 Barley Mow Passage, Chiswick, London W4 4PH
Tel: 081-994 6477

Council For The Care Of Churches
83 London Wall, London EC2M 5NA
Tel: 071-638 0971

Association for Studies in the Conservation of Historic Buildings
Institute of Archaeology, 31–34 Gordon Square, London WC1H 0PY
Tel: 071–387 6052

The British Architectural Library
66 Portland Place, London W1N 4AD
Tel: 071-580 5533

The last has a large collection of architectural drawings including numerous record drawings.

There are no extensive courses or formal specialist training generally available on the recording of historic buildings. Courses in the vernacular architecture of a region are sometimes available through adult education centres, and these will often include fieldwork through which participants can gain experience of the recording and interpretation of buildings of the kind visited. There are a number of local or regional building recording groups affiliated to the *Vernacular Architecture Group* (see above); participation in such a group can provide valuable experience through visiting buildings in the company of other members. Architects' knowledge of historic buildings varies greatly with the professional training that each has had, with the degree of their interest and with their experience thereafter. Some skilled building recorders, professional and amateur, have a professional background in architecture, but a great many have not (including the great majority of the staff of the Royal Commissions on Historical Monuments). All, whether a knowledge of historic buildings formed a part of their formal education or not, will have learnt most of their skills on the job, but the *Royal Commissions* may be prepared to accept people with a relevant background to accompany their field recorders and thereby learn something of the Commissions' approach and techniques.

An annual summer school concentrating upon practical experience in recording has recently been established, conducted jointly by the Royal Commission and English Heritage.

Courses in the care and conservation of historic buildings (both full-time and in some cases short courses), which though not specifically directed towards training in recording will include much that is relevant, are available to people with suitable previous training or experience at *Manchester University* (Department of Architecture); *York University* (Institute of Advanced Architectural Studies); and *The Architectural Association*, 34–36 Bedford Square, London WC1B 3EG.